TABLE OF CONTENTS

—

FOREWORD

—

Carl Chinn

As a young man was starting his career in law enforcement in the U.K., churches here in the U.S. were facing new challenges. Evil had invaded our sanctuaries with increasing frequency and intensity. By the end of the 20th century, we were seeing too many violent attacks on concentrated defenseless groups to ignore it anymore.

Since the dawn of time, there has been a roaring lion seeking to destroy those who worship God. He used to prowl like a shadow in the dark, but his attacks are now on display every day from the halls of Congress to the halls of our schools. He hates those who follow Christ with extra fervor. It isn't just bumping and bruising the heart that affects churches today. Lives have been taken and lives have been ruined by the immoral decay of the nation turned into violence in our most sacred places.

Responsible defenders across America were compelled to do something about it. As the pages turned from the 20th to the 21st century, we began to hear the term, "church security."

At first, it seemed a contradiction of terms to many and even dia-bolical to some. As scoffers scoffed, defenders defended. Endur-ing ridicule, lectures on passiveness, misrepresentation of scrip-tures (like "turn the other cheek") and cute little comments (like, "who would Jesus shoot?"), these defenders continue to protect.

However, the body count from deadly incidents, and the broken and shattered lives from sexual abuse in the church continued to pile up.

Church security emerged as sensible. It has been accepted by most level-headed faith-based leaders in the country. But something was missing.

Simon Osamoh was that young man in U.K. law-enforcement. His is a fascinating story of being brought to a new country, with skillsets and expertise for just such a time as this. While serving in the anti-terrorism efforts at the largest mall in America, he was asked one day to speak to a group of church security operators. He immediately identified what was missing.

He summed up the issue correctly in the pages following when he wrote, "places of worship needed a program to follow, something to guide them on this necessary endeavor." That statement is an arrow in the bullseye regarding our great endeavor.

It's said, "you can't judge a book by its cover." Like other metaphors, that isn't always true. I know Simon Osamoh. Simon lives like another man who was a warrior in a new land. Like Joshua 3,500 years earlier, the Lord brought Simon out and blessed him with the spirit of wisdom (Deuteronomy 34:9). The proclamation that "...as for me and my household, we will serve the Lord" (Joshua 24:15) is not just some nice wall decoration bought at a garage sale to Simon. It is a statement of his heart and it is the cover of everything Simon does, including this book. He passes his training and awareness onto the people he loves and to those he doesn't even know. It is to and for those who protect their friends and family who follow Christ and are targets of the same enemy.

Simon is altruistic in his mission. That is the kind of spirit that will help solidify what we do as responsible defenders of the faithful.

As Simon says, "when that day of evil comes, and it will appear somewhere in our faith community, you want to be ready."

This book will help you to be ready.

Carl Chinn

Founder & President
Faith Based Security Network

INTRODUCTION

—

I spent 14 years working as a detective with the British Police in England, concentrating on covert investigations into organized crime. I was honored to work on many high-profile international cases that included the 2006 liquid bomb terrorism plot, where British born Muslim extremists plotted against America to hijack planes. Following their arrest and prosecution, aviation security was changed worldwide by reducing the amount of liquids you can take on board planes. I was commended on eight occasions by the chief of police for my investigative work, respected by my peers, and saw myself as a 30-year officer climbing through the ranks. I did not see it at the time, but God had other plans for the gifts that He had given to me.

My family moved to America in 2011 and within a few weeks, I was overseeing counter-terrorism at Mall of America (MOA) in Minnesota. Some of you may know this as the largest shopping mall in North America covering over 6 million sq. ft. One day, a friend asked me if I could speak on suspicious behavior at their church. I hadn't spoken in front of a church group before or ever thought of bringing the security world I knew so well into places of religious worship, but as a Christian and a security professional, I thought "sure, why not". I presented for around 45 minutes to a group of ushers, greeters, and church staff. I felt out of my depth and slightly awkward, but I provided the effort the Lord provided the result. This team needed guidance in their security procedures.

They had question after question and that night it became clear to me that there was a real thirst for biblical security teaching. Since that night I have supported houses of religious worship in security education, security culture, how to get a safety team started, and how to implement safety programs. What I've found was that places of worship needed a program to follow and something to guide them on this necessary endeavor, which led me to create this very book. This 7-step guide has reached thousands of faith communities from many different denominations who all share the common goal of keeping their congregation and staff safe.

I am always impressed by the desire of church staff and volunteers to protect the people around them. These men and women balance faith, jobs, and family life with the time and effort it takes to run a safety program. You will hear me use the term security ministry throughout this book as that's exactly what safety and security is - a ministry. It should be treated no differently than the outreach programs or ministry work that your church is a part of. In my 20 plus years of working in public safety, I can tell you that to succeed in this area takes immense effort, dedication, and sacrifice.

One of the biggest issues that the church faces around the topic of safety is denial. Denial that there is a problem of crime and violence in worship settings (although the statistics show otherwise) and denial through scripture. Some just cannot believe that any harm will come to places of worship. As you read this book, you will learn that this is just not true. We must find ways to change the minds and culture surrounding security in a church. Scripture is not silent on personal safety and God portrays the world for what it is, broken. In both the Old and New Testament, we see violence through brokenness and sin.

The world we live in today is no different. You could argue that our generation has more human brokenness, more mental illness, more crime, and more mass shootings than past generations. While other targets are now being "hardened", churches remain "soft targets". A "soft target" would be an open-door church that has little or no security measures; easy pickings for motivated offenders to enter. Recent mass shootings have proven this point. In 2015, Dylann Roof, a white supremacist turned mass-murderer entered a weeknight Bible study at the Emanuel African Methodist Episcopal Church (AME) in Charleston, NC where he killed nine people including the senior pastor. A tragic event. As the story unraveled in the months after the incident, we learned that the church was not his intended target. Ironically, one of his friends who was an African American (and stated he had never seen racist behavior from Roof) told reporters that his intended target was a local school, but that the security there was too good for him to be able to carry out his attack. If you are a white supremacist wanting to kill black people and you cannot get into a school, what do you do? Well, Roof went to his next option. He chose arguably one of the most historic black churches in the country. He found doors open and an invitation to attend, which is exactly what he did.

My friend and respected church safety expert Carl Chinn (former building engineer at Focus on the Family in Colorado) was witness to a deadly force incident at his church where the assailant was killed in front of him by a member of their safety team. This changed him so deeply that he dedicated his life to collecting statistics on all deadly force incidents at houses of worship and has been doing so for over 20 years. This life-changing event led him to start the Faith-Based Security Network, which helps provide support for those in charge of church safety programs. His statistics are detailed, respected, and show a dramatic rise in deadly force incidents in American churches rising from 9 deaths in the year 2000 to 65 in 2016. While many factors could affect the rising trend of deadly force at faith organizations, I believe that there is a correlation between soft targets such as schools, hospitals, and sporting venues hardening their environment which has caused the displacement of motivated offenders to other suitable soft target locations such as churches.

The need for safety is not isolated to deadly force incidents.

Churches around the country have become event centers, places of mass gatherings, focal points in the community, and landlords to other nonprofits or small businesses. Places of worship embrace human brokenness and open their doors, believing that there is no sin that God cannot forgive. It is key to remember that most non-faith organizations do everything possible to keep this brokenness out of their buildings to keep their staff and visitors safe. Brokenness can lead to negative behaviors, and those behaviors can equal risk which we must either manage, mitigate, or hold onto, but in some way must address.

Faith communities are often ill-prepared with what society throws at them in terms of conflict. There is an increased moral and social responsibility that comes with having a building where members of the community attend. There is an expectation to keep children safe, help those who suffer from mental illness, abusive relationships, and sexual abuse, tackle suspicious behavior, radical and religious ideology, and so much more. When you add the attraction of technology, a cash-intensive business, expensive recording equipment, and computers out on display, the opportunity for a crime to occur increases.

Over the years I have lost count of the number of churches I have interacted with. I started to write this book when I discovered that churches needed guidance on how to create a safety plan. Although my views on biblical security and principles as a Christian are sprinkled throughout this book, the teaching is not unique to the church or a certain faith community and anyone concerned with their organization's safety will find value in following these steps.

As you read through, I believe you will see pieces of your story in every chapter. Take the key principles and apply them to your faith community. The suggestions I make come from my experience working with churches and places of worship to help make their ministry successful. Security is neither convenient nor inexpensive, but I hope to help you make informed decisions on how you can grow your security ministry and allow your environment to remain open and welcoming. What is essential is that you consider each step, identify where you are, and act. Only through action will you be able to build a strong safety program. My wish is that you follow these steps in order. Some of you might have already started your journey, so you may see some overlap. What's most important is that you review each step.

My prayer is that the Lord has used the skills and experiences He has provided me with as a tool to help develop your ministry and guide you in a time of need.

The horse is prepared for the day of battle, but victory belongs to the Lord

PROVERBS 21:31

STEP ONE

—

Identify Your Security Culture

—

The name of the Lord is a strong tower; the righteous runs into it and is safe

PROVERBS 18:10

Understanding the security culture of your organization is the best way to ensure the success of any safety program that you will implement. When I consult with faith-based organizations, the first question I ask is, "what is your church culture around safety?" Often, the response is "well, what do you mean?" What I mean by this is that it's important to understand how your church leaders feel about security. Would they want to carry guns? Are they open to training? What areas in the church need heightened security? When you begin to create a program you first need to understand the foundation you are starting on in order to grow and develop the program. It will be almost impossible to get any safety measures in place if you do not have the support of your religious leaders or business administrators so you need to know your church culture.

How can you improve worship safety if your religious leader does not know that there is an opportunity to do so? How can you efficiently tackle suspicious behavior if your staff and congregation think it is going against their faith values to report the breaking of social boundaries? Some people have the view that security is an expensive waste of time or even worse, that you have a sophisticated security program full of excellent policies and procedures, but no one follows them.

What is the response of your organization on things such as unattended items or suspicious behavior? Will someone knock on your office door to inform you that they have seen something that appears out of place? Will they tell you they have seen someone wandering around the church for 20 minutes going in and out of classrooms acting suspiciously? You could have the best policy writer on your team, but if the policy is not followed and the security culture is not proactive, the procedure is worthless. You need to understand what the security culture is in your environment.

In reading the last few paragraphs, you will have already formed an opinion of the security culture at your organization. Perhaps the names of individuals or departments come to mind who may not be in support of your safety program. Running a safety program is vast, time-consuming, and can quite often leave you feeling overwhelmed with how big the task is. Understand that security is a no end state. To be successful, you need the support of all ministries when making decisions focused on ministry safety. Knowing your security culture before you get started will provide you with a strong starting point, show you where the work needs to begin, and give you an idea of the journey you have ahead of you.

Here is an example as to why you need to know your security culture before you start developing a safety program. A pastor once told me that he was at a seminar when a pastor from a neighboring church asked him "Why do you have a safety team at your church, is something wrong?" The pastor told me he didn't feel he handled his response very well. He froze, spluttered out a few words, and came away feeling embarrassed that he hadn't thought about how he would answer this question. Not every pastor should know about all the security measures at their church, but the security culture starts with them. If you are asked a challenging question, remember you are not alone. Jesus faced many difficult situations as Mark 1:23-24 portrays, [23] "Just then there was a man in their synagogue with an unclean spirit; and he cried out, [24] "What business do we have with each other, Jesus of Nazareth? Have You come to destroy us? I know who You are - the Holy One of God!" Jesus was preaching in a synagogue when a man disturbed by the devil yelled out to him. If it can happen to the son of God, do you think this could happen at your church? And in John 7:1 it reads [1] After these things Jesus was walking in Galilee, for He was unwilling to walk in Judea because the Jews were seeking to kill Him. This scripture tells us that Jesus foresaw danger and acted. He acknowledged the harmful intent and avoided it.

FINDING YOUR CULTURE

To find the security culture of your church you must inquire about the perception of risk and response in your environment from the religious leaders, staff, and volunteers. After holding these conversations, you may find that views differ depending on the role of the person in ministry. It's not always easy to have these conversations but getting started is key. You don't want to embarrass them or put them on the spot. They may become defensive or feel challenged if it is perceived that the answer provided is insufficient. I get it, this is a tough job, and everyone is doing their best, but be very cautious. You are here to help, not criticize. Learning the cultural environment will later allow you to create a pathway to success.

Having done this many times in different faith denominations, the key is to identify a list of all individuals that you speak to and conduct private meetings to raise their safety awareness. Seek their views on risks and current security processes, and work to obtain their support. Churches were once seen as sacred and immune from crime, but the modern world is very different. Most houses of worship are soft targets meaning they have little or no security in place and by the very nature of your programs, actively invite risk into your building. Go into the conversations with an open mind, use statements such as:

» I'm reviewing security and ministry operations at the church and wanted to get your views.

» We want to improve our emergency resilience in (fill in the blank)...What can we do in your worship area to make you feel more secure?

» How would you respond if you saw something suspicious or unusual?

» What keeps you up at night?

» What would you like to see us implement at the church?

» When was the last time your department practiced a safety drill?

» How would you define our security culture?

Notice how the questions are taken from the "who, what, where, when, why, and how" family, designed to open a conversation and build rapport. At this stage, do not become concerned if safety gaps are starting to emerge, you just want to obtain views of the people around you. Do they acknowledge that crime in churches exists? Are they concerned about risk? Will they be responsive to procedural changes that affect their area? Will they attend training and be engaged? Make sure to record these conversations and take notes so you can reference them later.

Don't be surprised if you get a variety of responses. Some may give you an extensive list of things that keep them up at night and tell you how vulnerable they feel (most commonly from the facilities, front desk, and preschool staff). Others may say they have no worries at all and have never known anything bad to happen and that God will protect them, but often you find in the same breath they proceed to tell you story after story of security-related incidents. All these conversations help you better understand your environment and will help identify priorities at later steps in this process.

PREPARING FOR THE MEETING

You should prepare for this meeting with your religious leader well in advance. You must do your research and cover the basics of safety as this could be a new concept for them. Leaders are already swamped with attending seminars, responding to emails, and writing sermons. To lighten their load, let them know you "got this" and that a safety plan is being developed in the background. You are there to find their views and ideas, not to deliver them a problem. Make it clear you have the solution. I find most leaders are incredibly grateful to have a full overview of what's going on, which often ends the conversation with "I had no idea. Thank you for the insight, how can I help?" Or better yet, "I see you have this topic covered thank you."

Find two or three recent safety case studies involving a similar faith community or in your local area. If you google "church shooting", "church burglary", "child exploitation" or whatever issues you feel you should raise to the leaders, I'm confident you will find hundreds of articles from across the country. It's important that you provide a varied and well-balanced overview. If it's all about guns and deadly force, they may challenge the odds of this happening to your faith community or just think you want a gun. Keep your cases to the most common topics such as child sexual misconduct, embezzlement, domestic abuse, and acts resulting from mental illness.

Describe real-life incidents and show them that it could happen right here in our church! Some people have the mentality of, well that's in London, it would never happen here. Or that's in a small rural town in Texas it wouldn't happen to us in a big city. Statistically, the chance of winning the U.S. weekly Powerball lottery is 1 in 292 million, almost impossible you might say. Yet each week someone defies those odds and wins. Mass murderers such as Dylann Roof could walk through your door. At some point, it will happen to someone. How would you respond if this happened to you? You may remember the events at Sutherland Springs, Texas in November of 2017. I've had the honor to interview Frank Pomeroy, the pastor at the First Baptist Church. 26 people were killed that day and 20 seriously wounded. Frank's daughter was murdered at the hands of the gunman. When I spoke with Frank about the incident he said that a few days before the incident he was having dinner with some other pastors (he was away from the church the day of the incident) and the subject of safety came up. He told the pastors that he doesn't need security as he was just a small church in rural Texas. He told me he thinks of that conversation often and how he was in denial.

Present crime trends and statistical data to support your statements. Write a brief outline of how you would like the conversation to go and even put together a short PowerPoint presentation that you can refer to, either printed or on-screen. Write out your objectives as to what it is you want to get out of the meeting and practice the key points. Get a peer, your partner, or a friend to ask you some tough questions as you practice. Don't worry about having the right answer, often there isn't one, but having an answer that is well thought out is the goal to strive for in church safety. If tough questions arise, you can turn them back to your leader by saying "that's a good question, what do you think about that?"

I normally start conversations with the children's ministry, cutting straight to the chase. Vulnerable people, reputational concerns, and legal safeguards are at the top of anyone's mind in today's world when it comes to protecting children. These conversations generally lead to easier conversations on background checks, budgets, and training staff.

The purpose of the meeting is not to get a leader to commit and make decisions right there and then, but more so to help you better understand their direction, thought process, and views on security to help you understand the culture. Don't view this as one meeting to get it all out. Take your time, find a day on your leader's calendar when this conversation allows the time, focus, and energy it needs. If you're talking with the right people, push when needed, retreat when appropriate. This conversation will identify your path forward. You might not like what they have to say, but you'll know your culture, and this becomes your starting point to a stronger, safer environment.

NOTES

....

....

....

....

....

....

....

....

....

....

....

....

....

....

STEP TWO

—

Implement a Safety Committee

—

Commit your works to
the Lord And your plans will
be established

PROVERBS 16:3

Always remain in touch with the Lord and believe your prayers will be answered. Jim Theis is the Facilities and Security Director at my church (Westwood Community Church, MN) and I believe we met through his prayers. One day I was speaking to Brian Suter, one of the pastors at my church as we were picking up our kids who attended the same daycare. I told him of my background, my work at MOA, and asked who was overseeing safety at the church and to let me know if I could help. This message must have been relayed to Jim almost immediately as the following day he reached out saying that he had prayed for guidance and help on the safety team and then Brian had come into his office and told him about me. Those who don't share our same faith may call that a coincidence but given my background and expertise in security and the need at our church, it brought us together in a way that only God can. Jim had been praying and I felt a God prompting to talk with my pastor on security that day, knowing my experiences could help others. Jim and I have been good friends ever since. Now, not all God promptings lead to immediate action, but the power of prayer is strong. God takes everyday people with unique gifts and puts them together to bring glory to His name. The point to my story here is that this journey cannot be completed alone. You'll need friends to offer support, experts in the field, and a safety committee to assist you.

When I first moved to America, I had a fantastic opportunity to oversee counter-terrorism at MOA. People in the Mid-West know that this is America's largest shopping mall and entertainment complex where approximately 42 million people visit each year. People often ask how everyone is kept safe at MOA. Well, they have a strong security culture amongst staff in all safety aspects, they are incredible at collaboration, and they have interdepartmental support where all departments have representation on the safety committee. This committee shares the common goal of keeping the mall safe.

The idea of a safety committee is to gather individuals from different areas of the church with a common goal of supporting safe worship. Most faith-based organizations have just one person who oversees safety and security (for most churches this is a volunteer) so a strong collaborative effort is required to succeed and be able to influence change.

The functions of the safety committee can be decided by your newly appointed group as each church is different. The committee should discuss topics such as policy and procedures, training opportunities, current events, special events such as vacation bible school (VBS), reputational risk, and most importantly, discuss security incidents that may have occurred at your worship center. You can define what this committee looks like to you, but the goal here is to find a group of people that can come alongside you to support security ministry, discuss change, and influence all things safety-related.

When incidents happen, either those that you hear about in the media or those that happen at your church, the safety committee should come together and work through the situation by conducting an 'after-action' assessment. They will look for lessons learned and identify best practices to make necessary changes. Questions to review can be:

1. Who needs to be notified of the incident?

2. If this incident happened here, what would we do?

3. Do we have appropriate procedures in place?

4. What do we need to change?

5. What would stop this from happening again?

6. How do we educate the church?

This type of practice would be useful before incidents occur. Knowing that the church has mission trips to Africa or the Middle East or an upcoming VBS event with hundreds of kids; what does this mean in regards to safety? This would be a great time to discuss things like background checks and make proposals to the church board. There is strength in numbers; having a committee bring suggestions to decision-makers has more of an impact than just one person going at it alone.

WHO SHOULD BE ON THE COMMITTEE?

When Jesus started his journey into ministry he did not do it alone. To fulfill his father's wishes he had disciples join him. Jesus selected them one by one, each with a unique story to tell. Together they made a formidable team and as we know, took the gospel far and wide. He didn't take volunteers, he selected each person based on their unique gifts. This is the message I pass on to people at churches and faith organizations. Spend time to identify what gifts you need to make your committee a success and then go out searching for those that possess those gifts and talents. Within your church leadership board, you will have a great depth of experience, perhaps not in safety but in operations, finance, project management, and leadership which are all key attributes that are needed to grow your security ministry.

Regular meetings by the committee are essential. Remember, the goal is to provide direction and drive change. I've found that security ministry can lose focus if there are not formalized committee meetings. I would suggest that even if there are only small outstanding actions from a previous meeting or no actions at all, you still meet. It builds accountability and keeps your program focused on the mission to protect worship and make your church a safer environment. I have visited numerous churches where they have a clearly laid out plan and are incredibly enthusiastic in making a change for the better but cannot get the safety program off the ground. The root cause of this is often found to be the lack of accountability, little support, and no common goal amongst the staff. Let's look at some of the groups that would make good additions to your worship safety committee.

CHURCH LEADERSHIP

It doesn't matter if you are a church of 100 people or a mega-church with 4,000. Do your very best to try and identify a church leader who is willing and more importantly has the time to be a member of your safety committee. More than likely, your senior pastor won't have the time, but you should be able to find someone on the pastoral staff who can spare a few hours here and there to represent the leadership. This is beneficial for a few reasons, not only do they have the circle of influence with the trustees, executive committee, and other pastoral staff, but they will provide your committee with legitimacy. The world is changing around us. Those in administration roles such as business administrators, finance officers, and operations directors are being drawn more and more into areas of safety and can be the key to success. Even in small churches, if you find those that hold positions that involve risk, they will see the need for a safety committee. It's not always clear to us, but leaders do understand that it's important to protect our reputation, risk, and culture. I have spoken to numerous business administrators, spoken at pastoral seminars and facilities meetings and once the presentation is over, the offline questions come. "Thanks for helping us understand suspicious behavior, but what is the liability if something happens? Who is responsible?" These questions always tell me they get it, they understand the risk, but don't always know how to respond, take action, or even communicate with you that they understand. Having a church leader in a key role on your committee will increase the opportunity to influence change and improve security culture.

I have a story that shows the influence of how having someone in business administration on your committee can have a powerful impact. Some people still don't think this story is true, but I promise you it happened, and I'll tell you exactly how. I was supporting a church that could seat over 3,000 people. They host several services a day which meant there were at least 5,000-9,000 people in and out of their doors at the end of all the services on a typical Sunday. It would be considered a megachurch by most people's standards. The church wanted support in training staff and volunteers. It got to that awkward topic that no one likes to bring up... budget! I asked how much of a budget they had for training and the reply was "this year our total budget is 7". This number didn't concern me as I thought I knew what they meant; $7,000. I asked if the $7,000 was the budget just for training. "No Simon, $700 for the year is our total security budget". I just couldn't believe a church hosting over 9,000 people on a Sunday could align a $700 yearly budget for all security. I walked straight to the business administrator's office and in a very polite way, explained that this would not be acceptable and that they needed to join the safety committee. I can report they did both. The funding was given to facilities to run a comprehensive safety program and they joined the committee providing immediate legitimacy and support for the exhausted, frazzled facilities manager who had been trying to tackle safety on their own.

As you read this, a few people may have popped into your head about who you could approach to be on your safety committee. You know who would be a good fit to help you on this journey. Spend some time in prayer to find which disciple to approach, a lot is accomplished by asking through prayer.

FACILITIES STAFF

Facilities staff are most commonly the first line of defense for all things safety and security at your church. If people don't know how to do something, they call facilities. If a suspicious person or unattended item is found, people call facilities. If It's 2 pm on a Friday and someone doesn't know how to turn off the water and the facilities team have gone home, well guess what; that manager is getting a call at home asking where the shutoff valve is for the water.

If you work in facilities and have that feeling of being overwhelmed, you are not alone. When I visit different churches, facilities staff often tell me how they feel vulnerable, unprotected, unsupported, and untrained by the church in how to be security stewards of the building. These gallant people should be on your safety committee. Above all else, they get and understand feeling vulnerable, overwhelmed, and are often the people that get called when things go wrong in safety and security.

CHILDREN AND YOUTH WORKERS

This next group should be close to the top of your list when it comes to asking people to be on your safety committee. Jesus said, "Let the children alone, and do not hinder them from coming to Me; for the kingdom of heaven belongs to such as these. "(Matthew 19:14). Those that work with children have a vested interest in keeping them safe. Preschool directors, managers, and support staff know the risks around working with children. There are state requirements they must follow, and they tackle the questions from parents regularly on the topics of safety and security. No matter the size of the church, the questions parents have are "what is your policy on an active shooter?" "How often do you conduct background checks?" "How safe is my child?" Often preschool and childcare leaders have concerns of their own as to what keeps them up at night. They feel a huge depth of responsibility that comes with protecting God's children and need to be involved in the church's safety program.

The message here is to approach the departments that have a vested interest in a safe building, organization, and culture. You would think that includes everyone but remember in worship not everyone sees the world as you do, some are in denial, some are too busy, and some do not believe it is biblical. It would be no surprise to you that safety is not often the top priority of every ministry group.

PUBLIC SAFETY BACKGROUNDS

People that hold positions such as police officers, security professionals, risk and compliance managers, and emergency professionals often have the skills that you are looking for and are a great fit for this committee. Although working in public services is different from working in worship safety, in many ways it is similar with a crossover of skills and mission. The common denominator is collaboration, safety, and partnership.

I first got involved in security ministry because someone asked. A police officer friend asked me to go to his church and present to the ushers and greeters on suspicious behavior. This led to a call from another church, then another church, and then it became clear this was my calling. There are people with amazing skills hidden within the corners of our communities.

A word of caution when approaching public safety professionals, some people who work in public safety are known to do 'double duty'. Safety and security is part of their day job as well as their volunteer role at their place of worship. Be mindful when approaching people you know who work in public safety as they may not want to get involved. It can be hard for them to volunteer their time as it's "never a break from work". If they do say no, that's ok. Police officers, EMTs, and those that work in public safety often work long unsociable hours and they are fighting for time with their families as well to worship. They might not be keen to take on a role which means more time away from their family to help out on your committee. Remember, pray and the Lord will provide. Be transparent with them and make it clear that anything they can do, no matter how small, will be a support to your programs. In today's modern world they might not have to physically come to your meetings but can call in via Skype or Zoom, making them more likely to say yes. Focus on the little things that they can do to support the committee without asking for a long-term commitment. This is all about finding the balance, but those in public safety have a wealth of experience to share that can help develop your security ministry.

UNLOCK YOUR CONGREGATION'S GIFTS

Your place of worship will have members of the congregation offering their time, skill, and talent in many areas of ministry. These could be doctors, nurses, project managers, CEO's, CFO's, leaders, teachers, sales reps, and administrators to name a few.

These are all unique and strong gifts, but could you see these skills being translated to security ministry? Being a strong leader is often about finding people with the right skills and talents. Steve Jobs, the founder of Apple Inc. said it quite simply, "I don't hire talented people so I can tell them what to do. I hire talented people, so they can tell me what to do". You know the mission and what you are looking to achieve. Members of your congregation may have gifts that have made them successful outside of the church that can be transferred to your safety committee, especially those in business continuity, planning, and project management. What better way to get this project off the ground than finding people with the right level of talent.

MEETING EXPECTATIONS

You've found the right people, sent the calendar invite, and you're waiting for people to attend the first meeting. At the first meeting, an expectation should be set as to how often the group should meet. Depending on the size of the church, it's best practice to get the group together bi-monthly. If you think you can meet more frequently, go for it, but bi-monthly is a good starting point. Remember, you'll be holding hours of discussions and you'll want people to own certain actions and report back at the next meeting. Bi-monthly is a suitable amount of time to hold a volunteer accountable for something they promised to do, and not too long should you need to play catch up. Let's face it, most of us in worship are volunteers and time is our biggest challenge, so you need to be realistic, but make sure people are held accountable for their actions.

Schedule out a series of meetings on people's calendars so they know the expectation for the year and can plan to attend. You are far more likely to get all of your committees to attend if you're giving a couple of months' notice. This helps maintain the momentum, ensure people are in attendance, and drive projects and actions forward.

When people call me and say they are struggling with this step, I normally find it is because the group is meeting too infrequently. The mentality of the meeting becomes 'we will meet when we can'. The meeting is pushed back and 'when we can' never comes. The meeting then eventually drops off the calendar and then stops altogether. It will be difficult to find a time that suits everyone due to the nature of people's day jobs and family time, but don't fall into the trap of trying to please everyone. You do have to think about what the key times are for your group to meet in order to remain successful. Skype and Zoom are great alternatives if someone can't physically attend.

You'll have scheduled meetings where you will draw on the experience of those around you to develop processes, procedures, best practices, and future direction of the program, but another key time to meet is after a safety incident has happened. As an example, it's 3 pm and the church is empty because it's Friday afternoon. An elderly volunteer is on the front desk when a man comes in asking for money. The church's policy is not to give out money, only food and vouchers for local shops. The man gets aggressive, scares the elderly volunteer, and leaves. When you first hear about this incident is the perfect time to call the committee together for an ad hoc meeting. Discuss what needs to be changed or what to do differently. How can your team best support the people on the front desk? Assign actions, arrange meetings with key stakeholders if needs be, and act. Five to six heads are better than one and you can consider how to improve safety measures on the front desk going forward. Another key time to meet is when a safety or security-related incident has occurred outside of your church, and you heard about it on the news or social media. Getting the team together to discuss how you would handle the same incident if it happened at your church will help you identify potential gaps in your current process and influence change.

CREATE A MISSION STATEMENT

A mission statement is a must for your safety committee. It will define the scope of responsibilities and outline what the committee is looking to achieve. Maybe you can relate to a time when you were on a committee without a defined mission and you became the dumping ground for everything. The goal is to be helpful, but not pick up all the 'tasks' people don't know what to do with. Your mission is to keep worship, staff, and volunteers safe within your culture; so, define it. At the beginning of your first meeting bring this up and brainstorm. Having a mission statement for your security ministry spells out the intent and provides direction. Some churches will use scripture, others a simple statement to define the mission. Perhaps something is already coming to mind and you have started to write down some notes. Create this as a team as it should align with the security culture and philosophy of the church. Don't forget the power of prayer. Time and prayer will provide a sense of clarity for you.

My last point is structure. Churches that have safety teams without a leader or no one in charge will find it extremely difficult to accomplish tasks. Like any committee, it will work best with structure and clearly defined roles. If you are the person in charge of the committee and chair the meeting, call it to order! Have someone take notes, provide accountability, assign actions, and lead discussions on priorities. You will have representation from different area ministry teams, and each brings a unique perspective. No doubt there will be strong opinions and personalities, so having someone 'in charge' to help navigate those conversations is essential. Remember as the leader to interject humility into the discussion. It shouldn't be a meeting to argue, but rather an open discussion to evaluate best practices and establish future guidelines. Establishing the foundation for guideless is important because you always train to the guidelines. Initially, you might have more questions than answers, but you are in it together and over time you will be able to look back and see how much you've accomplished.

NOTES

....

....

....

....

....

....

....

....

....

....

....

....

....

....

....

STEP THREE

—

Protect your Perimeter

—

But we prayed to our God,
and because of them we set
up a guard against them
day and night

NEHEMIAH 4:9

The protection of a perimeter is the foundation of any security program. This is no different in ministry operations. Protecting your perimeter is often a simple and relatively inexpensive way to protect yourselves. The truth is that once you let a person with harmful intent past your perimeter you are already at a disadvantage. Unfortunately, spotting those with harmful intent is often the hardest part. In the Trojan War, a popular story in the mythology of ancient Greece, a Greek King held the city of Troy under siege for 10 years to save a woman who had been kidnapped by a Trojan Prince, but they could find no way to penetrate the city gates and tried year after year to get into the city. They decided to trick those inside the gates to open them up by leaving the gift of a giant wooden horse outside. The horse, filled with soldiers waiting to attack, was led inside the city gates. Once the horse was taken inside, the soldiers began to attack. The people behind those city gates were at a disadvantage because the perimeter was penetrated.

In safety and security, it can be easy to become complacent. Here is a personal example from my neighborhood. In just one night, 10 homes were broken into and two cars stolen from driveways. The following day, the events that transpired overnight were the talk of the neighborhood. How were people able to come in the dead of night, break into 10 houses and steal two cars? The reality was that the neighborhood became complacent in basic security practices and left their doors open and cars unlocked. They became sitting ducks and rich pickings for motivated offenders who took advantage of complacency. I recall hearing comments such as "this is a quiet neighborhood" and "this has never happened here before." I also remember seeing the embarrassment on my neighbor's faces as they realized that they had allowed these motivated offenders to just walk past their perimeters without challenge. Just the simple act of locking their doors would have made it difficult to enter and would have been a deterrent to the offender. Interestingly, the ones who locked their doors were not victims of crime that night.

ISIS CHURCH ATTACK, SAINT -ETIENNE-DU-ROUVRAY, FRANCE

In July of 2016, two teenage boys walked into a small Catholic church in the French town of Saint-Etienne-du-Rouvray around 40 miles west of Paris, France. It was a little after 9:00 am when Priest Jacques Hamel, age 86, was delivering the morning mass when he had his throat slit by one of the boys. He died almost instantly. The two attackers who were revealed to be Islamic terrorists, entered via an insecure rear door of the church shouting "Allahu Akbar" (meaning "God is the greatest"). Allahu Akbar has been shouted during several high-profile terrorist attacks where the attackers wish to be identified as an Islamic extremist group.

It was determined during the investigation that the attack was pre-planned. The church had been targeted before the attack and the attackers knew that the rear door to the church would be unlocked, giving them easy access. The attackers had conducted surveillance of the church and determined that the rear door was a vulnerability that they could exploit to gain entry. Unfortunately, this vulnerability is no different to hundreds of churches across the country who leave their doors open, creating a welcoming atmosphere for everyone. This should serve as a warning to all of us. While we all wish to create a loving and welcoming environment for worship, all entrances must either have a staff member to greet people at the door, or the doors should be locked and secure. The goal is to funnel people who enter your church past a person who can welcome them and at the same time foresee any danger. Keeping multiple entrances open to your church and allowing free access prevents you from knowing who is in your building, which is a basic security principle. We want to be able to foresee danger and take action. You cannot do this if people have full access and you do not even know they are present.

The unfortunate reality in today's world is that we simply cannot become complacent with foundational security practices. We can no longer leave our doors open at night or hop out of our car for a few minutes when we run into the convenience store without locking it. In places of worship, there is often high-value video equipment, computers, and musical instruments out on display. Many churches use the statement "all are welcome here" in their advertising. We must constantly challenge ourselves as to what this statement means in our faith communities. It's not that I do not believe in having open door churches where all are welcome, but the risk involved in providing open access is becoming greater and greater. Our doors are open for those that want to seek sanctuary, come to faith, or learn about how to build a relationship with God. Those that come to our churches such as the gunman in Sutherland Springs who killed 26 and South Carolina who killed nine, would not have been welcomed by those faith communities had they known their intent. Having multiple entry points left open is a vulnerability that becomes a risk. You do not need to "lockdown" your sanctuary, just ask yourself a simple question; do I always know who is on the premise? If you have six entrances to your church, can you close four so that people who enter are directed past a member of staff or a volunteer? The next task is then very simple; greet the person with an open question. Say something like "Good morning, how can I help you?" or "What brings you to the church today?" It is very important to greet people as they enter. Like in the story of the Trojan horse, your perimeter is being breached every time someone walks in. Asking these questions allows you to either minister to them or find out why they are there.

During an assessment of a church, I went to see where the pre-school area was and discovered it was in a far wing of the building, with all the offices and welcome desk at the other side. I saw at least three separate entry points that led from the street directly into the preschool area, making it possible for people to enter without being seen by a member of staff. The location of these doors made it almost impossible for teachers to know who was in parts of the building during preschool hours. Unless there is a building code regulation that prohibits it, it's essential to guide all people who enter the building past a member of your team. Knowing who is around your high-risk areas or any other ministry focal points (such as children) should outweigh the desire to have a door unlocked and accessible.

SOFT TARGETS!

Churches are considered soft targets, but a person or ministry group can also be considered a soft target. In terms of buildings, churches have historically been deemed soft due to their vulnerability in being unprotected and having little or no security measures in place, sometimes referred to as a "sitting duck". The term "target hardening" simply means making your building less vulnerable to risk. It's similar to how you would install an alarm system, a dog warning sign, or cameras to your home to imply that you take security seriously by hardening your environment. Hard targets are places that have restricted access and have robust security measures in place such as airports, government buildings, and courtrooms. When considering your perimeter, it's natural to start with the building, but it's important to think of the surroundings as well. For most urban churches it starts with the parking lot. It's common for urban churches in and around city centers to have issues with youth presence in their parking lots resulting in crime such as car theft and drug dealing. Church location can also determine your risk factor. Geographical location can make you a hard target and a soft target. For example, if I am the pastor at a downtown church right next door to the police precinct, I am a harder target as my geographical location means the police response time will be quicker. If I am in a small rural church with little or no police department, my location could make me a softer target as possible intruders know there will not be a quick response. Some questions to think about, where does your perimeter start and how is it secured overnight? What can you do to improve your perimeter?

DON'T OVERLOOK SIMPLE THINGS!

When it comes to securing your perimeter don't overlook standard practices such as checking doors, locks, and windows to ensure that they are doing their intended job. When I walk around church buildings conducting security assessments, I often find doors propped open, broken, or inoperable locks, and large stones waiting on the ground for that motivated offender to throw through a window. Often, I see that church windows are left open, which makes them susceptible to random acts of theft and vandalism. Try to consider your doors and windows a perimeter that someone is trying to breakthrough. How effective will the security measure be? Simple fixes can dramatically improve your safety.

Create a simple checklist for staff to ensure those outside stones are removed and ground floor windows are locked when the last person leaves for the day. The checklist doesn't have to be long but find a way to make it hard for a motivated offender to enter your building. This will also help identify areas that can be improved inexpensively such as installing security film to your exterior and interior windows which prevents the glass from shattering.

IMPROVE LAYERS OF SECURITY

A common way to improve your perimeter protection is through increasing or strengthening the layers of security often referenced to as "layers of security" or "circles of security". This is a method of protecting your environment using different layers (preventative security methods) against a specific threat. The goal is to devise a security plan to prevent a person from coming into your church to carry out deadly force. By training ALL of your staff on suspicious behavior, red flags, and empowering them to make informed decisions on reporting, you are improving a layer of security designed to address suspicious behavior.

Here's an example of how the layers work together. A person enters carrying an unusual item. All of your staff and volunteers are trained to notice this behavior; therefore, you already have an inherently safer environment as you have multiple reporters looking for the same threat. In this scenario, the greeter on the front door is welcoming someone new to the church. In doing so, they miss the person who walks past them carrying a large bag, which is unusual at this church. The usher, who is outside the worship center handing out programs, immediately spots the person and knows this is breaking a social boundary (and unusual). They radio for a safety team member who sees the person and approaches them. They conduct a conversational interview and find out that the bag is full of old clothes that will be donated to the church after the service. As with most suspicious behavior, there generally is a reasonable explanation. Each person in this story is a layer of security that helps prevent against the specific threat of suspicious behavior. The greeter (layer one) did not see the unusual activity but the usher (layer two) did and was able to take action. The safety team member (layer 3) was trained in conversational interviewing and could find the person's intent with the bag. A security program based on multiple layers is always the strongest as no one layer is infallible.

What are the layers of security at your church or buildings? What can you do to introduce more or improve the layers of security that you already have? When off-campus activities are taking place, ensure that there are certain layers of safety for those events happening as well. Improving simple things can make all the difference.

KEEP VOLUNTEERS IN PLACE

Protecting your perimeter requires both the role of 'guard' and 'watchman'. That is exactly what Habakkuk and Ezekiel were in the Old Testament, spiritual watchman warning the people of Israel about God's judgment. The Lord calls upon us to do the same, be a watchman. In 1 Peter 5:8, scripture tells us "Be of sober spirit, be on the alert. Your adversary, the devil, prowls around like a roaring lion, seeking someone to devour." We are to watch, warn, and educate people of the dangers no matter how much adversity we face. An attack is always imminent.

As I've mentioned, your most important perimeters to protect are your doors. The greeters are the first point of contact for someone entering the church and are a layer of security that can welcome guests as well as spot potential harm. There can be a temptation to remove the greeters from your church doors once the service has started, which leaves your perimeter unattended. Have your greeters stay in post all through the service. I've attended so many churches where the greeters are at the doors doing all the right things, shaking hands, fist bumps with little kids, serving the community whilst keeping a watchful eye over the flock. It's one of the things I love about my church, it is almost impossible to walk in on any given day of the week without multiple people greeting you, but I also see lots of churches where the greeters vacate their door assignments five minutes after the service has started. The mentality is 'job done, next assignment', but this leaves the church vulnerable to someone walking in a few minutes later wanting to cause harm. Those are the very people the Lord is calling us to save. Suspicious behavior is not just something we report, but minister to. Keeping people on the doors during your service serves a dual purpose.

A WIDER PERIMETER

A couple of years ago I attended a Sheepdog seminar run by Jimmy Meeks. I had the opportunity to meet Carl Chinn, founder of Faith Based Security Network (FBSN), and we quickly became good friends. Retired Lieutenant Colonel Grossman spoke about the Sandy Hook tragedy (December 14, 2012) where 20 children and 6 staff were killed at the hands of an active shooter. Generally, after these mass killings come the lawsuits, and Sandy Hook was no different. The victims' families either reached financial settlements or held court action. Grossman focused his presentation on why the Sandy Hook families were able to bring lawsuits against the school district. One of the reasons appeared to be so simple; some of the classroom doors were unable to be easily locked. Some of the doors had to be locked from the outside, and during a high-stress situation, some of the teachers could not perform what would seem like an easy task to keep the children safe. It is medically proven that when under high situational stress, you can lose your ability to perform 'simple' tasks, such as locking a door. When under immense pressure, these fine motor skills can diminish. Also, think about programs such as your children's areas. Can they be locked down independently from the rest of your building? Some large churches have entire wings that can be locked down. Not everyone has the funds or building design to do this but reflect on the high-risk areas of your church and consider internal perimeters and how you might secure them.

As we start to look at security more holistically, here are a few examples of what might be included in a wider perimeter:

» The area that surrounds your church

» Parking areas and ramps

» Walls, fences, shrubbery

» Church-owned buildings on your land

» Stairs and sidewalks that enter the building

» Doors, windows, roof

» Internal perimeters (staff rooms and offices, preschool and designated child nursery areas, money storage areas)

» Money storage areas and monetary transportation routes

SOME FINAL WORDS!

The world around us has changed and protection of your perimeter is a top priority. When you hold mass gatherings, the doors should always be manned by your volunteers. This is good for security and customer service by giving that open-door feel while making sure you are doing everything you can to protect your perimeter. Not all churches can afford high-end security systems and security cameras, but if you have cameras and are using them to protect your perimeter, make sure that all entrances are covered. Make sure the cameras are close enough so someone can see body language and clothing not just a blob on a screen that looks like it could be a person. Cameras are only proactive if someone is going to watch them during your hours of operation, otherwise, they are a reactive tool, only useful after the fact. Appoint someone to observe your cameras and focus on the doors. Like in the trojan horse scenario, we are trying to find those motivated offenders at the point of entry. If you are lucky enough to have a safety team, make the person on your cameras be your dispatcher. All you need is someone with a keen eye for detail who knows your church culture and is a good communicator.

NOTES

....
....
....
....
....
....
....
....
....
....
....
....
....
....
....
....
....
....
....
....
....
....
....
....

STEP FOUR

—

Conduct a Security Assessment

—

The prudent sees the evil and hides himself, But the naive go on, and are punished for it

PROVERBS 22:3

When starting a safety program there is often a desire to jump straight towards implementing a safety team. This can cause most people to overlook perhaps the most crucial thing that can determine the success of your program, conducting an assessment of your current security practices. You will hear many terms for a security assessment such as risk assessment, threat assessment, vulnerability assessment, or security audit. Although different terminology, they all pretty much have the same meaning; assessing your threat profile, the current state of security controls, and your ability to respond. Assessments are intended to help identify program strengths, ineffective security measures, and assist in creating a road map to enhancing your teams, processes, and technology.

There are many reasons why a security assessment will benefit your security program. One is to provide an improvement road map from point A to point B that you can easily follow. However, completing the assessment is only the start of the process. Organizations need to find qualified individuals that can implement the identified recommendations and guide you through to the end of the process. Faith communities are expected to create and maintain a safe and welcoming environment and culture. Understanding the shortcomings of your safety program and creating a plan to improve security is essential to mitigate risk. As an employer and a place of public mass gatherings, there are rules that the law of the land requires us to follow. While these laws can conflict with our faith, scripture can help to provide us with guidance. Luke 20 is a great example when Jesus is being asked by the Pharisee on guidance for paying taxes to Caesar. [21] They questioned Him, saying, "Teacher, we know that You speak and teach correctly, and You are not partial to any, but teach the way of God in truth. [22] Is it lawful for us to pay taxes to Caesar, or not?" [23] But He detected their trickery and said to them, [24] "Show Me a denarius. Whose likeness and inscription does it have?" They said, "Caesar's." [25] And He said to them, "Then render to Caesar the things that are Caesar's, and to God the things that are God's." Luke 20:21-25.

We know the Pharisees were trying to trap Jesus, but He also provides us with a framework that can be applicable in how security ministry must operate today. Give to God what is God's and give to the law of the land what is the law of the lands. No matter our political beliefs, the law requires us to keep a safe environment. Jesus understood this and it's a reflection of his knowledge of a natural act versus a supernatural one. Conducting a security assessment to identify your risk and vulnerabilities is the recommended starting point and will allow you to find ways within your budget to take action. You don't know what you don't know. We want to know and understand everything and have a roadmap to be successful in our program.

GETTING STARTED

Most assessments start with identifying and ranking facility assets or the things that are most important to the facility e.g. people, money, building, and technology. This information is gathered during a review of your building and interviews with key staff members and volunteers. We will talk more about this process later.

Once a list of assets is created and prioritized, a list of potential threats that pose the greatest risks to your facility should be determined. These should be realistic events that could happen and adversely impact your location e.g. violence, theft, domestic disputes, natural hazards, and other incidents. Once this list is created, a list of protective measures (controls) designed to reduce the vulnerability to each threat should be created.

For example, a downtown church is widely known to offer cash to those in need of food and gas. Hundreds of dollars in petty cash is kept in one of the staff offices. The threat is that an assailant can take advantage of the church's generosity and come back to the church during the day and break into the office. Now that the risk is known, find security measures that limit this vulnerability. (1) Divert all door access during the day to one entry point where every person has to walk past a volunteer or staff member who will greet them (2) Provide the volunteer or staff member with a list of suspicious behaviors that you want them to report or escalate immediately. (3) The petty cash is moved to a more secure part of the building where visitors are not permitted (4) Implement a policy where a member of staff brings cash to the front area when requested so the person receiving the donation does not know where the money is stored (5) The door to the office is card access or key-controlled (6) Have a CCTV camera which is streamed to the desk of someone who monitors cameras.

Once the risk is identified (theft of church money) and several preventative measures (controls) are put in place, it will reduce the vulnerability to that risk. Fiduciary responsibilities are best accomplished with at least two people working in tandem to accomplish the goal. There is a skill and art form associated with this process but essentially you are recording the risk and evaluating or recommending preventative measures that make it less likely for that risk to become an actual event. As you start this journey you will need to think about what areas of the church the assessment should cover. It can cover all program operations but will become lengthy and complicated. Most churches are not equipped to handle an assessment that covers all programs, but that doesn't mean it can't be done. Here are a few suggested common areas that could be the focus of your assessment:

» Worship Services: Entrances and emergency exits, current plans for evacuation, fire, storms, and active shooter situations

» Technology: Access control, alarms (panic/burglary), video surveillance, etc.

» Security Procedures: Working with children, nursery procedures, background checks for specific ministry groups, response procedures, lockdown, fire, etc.

» Special Events: Outdoor baptisms, VBS, high profile speakers, private events, conferences, social functions, youth program activities, music concerts, large community-based activities, or off-campus group activities

» Physical Security: Doors, locks, alarms, protection of video equipment, valuables, protection of human asset

» Preschool Security: Building layout, sign in/sign out procedures, staff training, background checks

» Staff/Volunteer Training: Situational awareness, scenario training, policy procedures, EAP, Lockdown, medical, etc. (Include all hazards)

» Cash Handling: The use of modern technology to pass offerings and cash movement

» Vehicle Operations: Insurance coverage, fair use, driver policies

» Foreign Ministry Travel: Security assessments, insurance, K&R

policy (kidnap and ransom), medical coverage, business continuity planning, executive protection (EP), contract security.

» Building Activities: Alcoholic anonymous (AA), counseling services, domestic violence groups, mental health, chemical dependency groups, weddings, and funerals

» Drills: What type of emergency operations are being practiced regularly and how are the results being discussed and
recorded

In many organizations, I consider the following factors to help
prioritize new recommendations: fiscal cost, resource cost, risk re-
duction, and implementation time frame.

WHO SHOULD CONDUCT THE ASSESSMENT?
Who should conduct your security assessment is often the most
challenging question. You will need to weigh out your priorities of
budget, time, and treasure against your most desired outcome.
What do you hope to accomplish by having a comprehensive
assessment of your building, procedures, and technology? It's ok
to conduct this process yourself, but it's challenging. Do you have
the skills that make you the best person to do this? The size and
complexity of your organization will often drive who is best. I have
thoroughly enjoyed the experiences the Lord has put in front of
me; the national courses I have attended, the international audi-

ences I have presented to, and the high-profile safety positions I have held. They have equipped me with the skills and experience required to advise churches on best practices regarding safety. When considering a vendor, police officer, or person within your community, ask those challenging questions. Do they have the experience and skills to complete the task?

My many years of experience in law enforcement has taught me that police officers and detectives are not always physical security leaders. Most of the time they're highly trained reactive resources. A security assessment is a proactive holistic view of your program functions. A large percentage of churches I talk to mention a "retired cop" or "active cop" within their community who they are going to ask to do the assessment. The role of security and law enforcement is quite different. I'm not saying a police officer couldn't do the assessment, I've worked with some amazing crime prevention officers who do this very well, but my message here is do not assume police officers have the skills for this function. All that aside, your local police department is a fantastic resource.

Here is my advice on who should conduct your assessment. Write a list of requirements, needs, and wants then determine who has the skills to best fit your needs. It's similar to a job interview, you have the job description and your trying to find the best person to fill that role. Often there is a compromise, but your requirements should be the main focus. If your church has 50 people, the requirements probably dictate that you need more of an informal document that you can discuss with your church elders. If you have a church with 600 members, chances are you're in a larger building with more governance and accountability. You might need to provide a formal presentation to your church leadership and vote on who is the best fit for the job. Ask friends and other churches who they have worked with in the past. Conduct research to get a list of reputable companies, then conduct your due diligence, check references, interview the candidates, and request to see a sample of their work. Draw up a shortlist of those that align with your church culture. Work with your safety committee to help identify the one that has everything you are looking for, then make the selection. As a consultant, I am more than happy to share references and come on-site to show a sample of our work and you should expect this from anyone you work with. There are always compromises in this process, but I want to emphasize that I see many people make the wrong decision here. Either they go with someone who is not suitable, or they are unhappy with the outcome, so it doesn't help move their program forward. The key stage of vendor selection is due diligence. Here are some areas for consideration that will help you stay on course:

» Check references

» Have they worked with a church previously?

» Is the assessment a fixed price?

» Obtain a detailed proposal listing of all the things they will do

» What are the skills within their organization?

» What do Google reviews say? What is their online presence? What do you see on Yelp or social media?

» How long will the process take?

» Will they come back and present their recommendations to your church board?

» What support do they offer after the report is generated?

» Discussion of the report

The scope of the report should have been identified when you were building your requirements for the project so you should have a clear idea as to what you are expecting. If you have hired a consultant, will it be a 50 or 200-page document? If you go at it alone, how will you present recommendations to your church leadership? Don't take on a bigger report from a consultant than you can handle as you can leave unmitigated risk out there. Understand what it will look like before it is written. Remember your assessment is to evoke change, make enhancements to your program, and make the church safer.

To make sure you get what you need out of the report, I would sit down and consider these points and walk through each of them with the person conducting your assessment.

» Can you see a sample document?

» Will any upcoming building projects be included?

» How big will the final report be?

» How many hard copies will be provided?

» Will the soft copy be in word or PDF?

» Can recommendations be provided in a separate word document or excel for presentation?

» Will you see the document for a round of edits?

INTERVIEW KEY PEOPLE

To complete the assessment process, you will need to interview (hold conversations) to find out what a day at the church or building really looks like. The more detailed your conversations can be, the more accurate picture you will get of true security practices at the church. The second reason why you want to conduct interviews is that they will help guide the onsite assessment. You cannot possibly cover every program or every aspect of safety. If you do the report will end up being the length of The Bible and remember this process is to evoke change and make a difference. If the end-user of this report is overwhelmed then action will not be taken. So, these interviews are used to identify new or existing risks and help prioritize where energy should be focused on during the assessment.

I conducted a security assessment where the operations manager told me that they needed to improve the security culture. During the assessment, I interviewed several key volunteers who made the statement "can you make sure they take action this time and not just talk about it?" This message helped me determine where I needed to spend my time. Holding these conversations provides an accurate picture of the environment. No one had mentioned the lack of action at this church until I met with these volunteers. Volunteers often see what goes on in the day to day processes and can be the best resource for giving a thorough line of data for your analysis. The leaders were talking a lot but taking no action and people were skeptical. We would need to work on this skepticism through implementing a new security culture to ensure that change takes place. Most church campuses are multi-functional and have a variety of non-church related activities at various times of the day. I often use the phrases "all hazards" and "whole church security" as the focus on security should not solely be on worship days or times, but also focus on the business and tenants associated with the church.

There is no standard number of interviews to conduct, but it's fair to say you will get out of it what you put into it. If you're doing this yourself, talk with everyone. If you're hiring a consultant, agree on a fair number of interviews to conduct before they start as this is where many hours can be spent and time means expense. During the interviews, the purpose is to find out what is working, what needs improvement, and what the person is most worried about from their perspective. Remember different worship programs, tenants, and congregations all see risk differently. The preschool leader is going to have different concerns than an outreach leader or one of your church musicians. Start with, "when it comes to the safety of the church, what keeps you up at night?" Always ask open-ended, tell me, explain to me, describe to me, who, what, where, when, why, and how questions (these will be explained in further detail at a later point in the book). The interviewee should be doing 90% of the talking here. You will find that this will provide you with more conversation than you might have thought was out there. Here are some of the roles that will provide you with a good understanding of the day to day environment that you should consider asking these questions to:

» Key employees (ministry leaders/preschool /outreach programs)

» Key volunteers (ushers greeters etc.)

» Church Leadership (trustee/executive board/religious leaders)

» Facilities teams

» Business administration/Finance departments

» Tenants and third parties that use the building

» Congregation (select number)

The last guidance I would give on this topic is what you tell the interviewees. I tell them the information they provide is not linked to their name and the feedback might be edited so it can be shared, but this isn't always a catalyst for the best information. I conducted a security assessment at a school and interviewed 10-12 students about their perceptions of safety, attitudes of teachers, and if they knew of any breach in school policies. These were high school kids aged 15-17. I was an outsider and told them this is confidential and whatever you tell me will not have your name attached to it. Do you think they told me everything? Did they have immediate trust in me? No! This is ok as we've all been a teenager wary of when an adult says "it's ok you can trust me" only to be hauled up to the principal's office. So, at the end of our discussions, I gave them each a piece of paper, a pen, and a plain envelope. I said write down something that you haven't told me today about the school security or what goes on and put it in this envelope. From this process, I had ten times the response and was able to find gaps in the current security procedures.

Laying out the procedure at the beginning and being direct and clear will help the process. You could say something like "I need one hour of your time, please bring one or two good/bad examples of safety at the church and think about what you are most concerned with and what you would like to see changed. I will not be recording the conversation, but I will be taking notes. Anything you tell me will be confidential with no named attribution." Hopefully, you will be able to determine what works best in any given situation.

COMPONENTS OF AN ASSESSMENT

Once the interviews are complete, the collected information will help you identify areas to focus on during the assessment. You always want to be intentional and take things one day at a time. Ask yourself things such as, "what can I do today to move in the right direction?" "What are the things that will require me to move capital expenditure?" "What should we look to accomplish in the next two to five years?" During the assessment phase, I deploy a methodology that most commonly covers these four principal areas.

» People

» Physical Security

» Technology

» Process

People includes training, awareness of procedures, and skills required for job roles. Physical security covers your doors, locks, windows, lighting, and layout of your building. Technology review will cover things like cameras, alarms, card access, and mass communication methods. Process is one of the most crucial pieces of your safety program, as this is where controls (safety measures) start to fall short. Review documents such as policy and procedures, background requirements, vendor contracts, emergency action plans, and workplace violence prevention programs. You might find you don't even have any documents and you will start to identify vulnerabilities. This is where the list of recommendations will start to build. The objective is to offer solutions to the exposed vulnerabilities to increase your security effectiveness. Write down the four buckets (people, physical security, technology, and process) and place your current program within each of these categories. Take a methodical walk-through of your targeted processes. For each process, review the documentation, ask why it does or does not work effectively, and make assessments of the controls in your program.

The assessment should be well balanced. It is good practice to not only focus on the improvements but also capture the things that are going well and explain why. I call them "commendable elements" in my reports. A great way to do this is by providing a visual of good and working practices. There is always low hanging fruit in any assessment; those blocked fire doors, the absent slip mats on the concrete floors, and the stones left right by the door after someone used it to prop it open. Capture these stories in pictures. When conducting a security assessment, a camera phone is a person's best friend. I take hundreds of pictures not knowing what I will use but they become so helpful at the report stage. I conducted an assessment of a preschool where the emergency exit was blocked off. I could tell the business administrator that this was a violation of the law and a high risk, but the image was so impactful that the member of staff was actually disciplined as a result. The saying 'a picture is worth a thousand words' is true. It will bring your report alive and provide a helpful visual to the reader.

When reviewing physical security, you'll want to seek out consistency in how you approach and review the building. Utilizing a simple checklist will provide you the consistency required to generate an accurate assessment and ensure all relevant data points are covered. It's important that you understand what is happening in the building at different times of the day. As an example, the church will appear very different at 2 pm on a Tuesday as to what it looks like on a Sunday during service. A Sunday during service looks different than 8 pm on a Thursday when you have other activities taking place. Make sure your review takes into consideration the range of service times and outreach programs that will operate in your building to ensure everything is covered.

HANDING OVER THE REPORT

If you've hired a consultant and they have provided you with the report, make sure you understand each word, picture, recommendation before you share this with others especially if sharing on email. Once you share it with others you lose control of the document. People will have questions and so it is critical that you understand what the consultant is telling you before you share it. Once you are comfortable with the report, call a special meeting for your safety committee to discuss the recommendations. Most often people tack this onto the agenda of their normal business meeting, but it's best practice to discuss the report findings when it is the sole focus of a meeting to ensure there are no distractions and you have people's full attention. When I provide the final report to churches, I give them some time to reflect on the recommendations before I re-engage with them. This can be as little as a few days up to a couple of months to allow them to digest the contents. Then I come back and present the findings to the church leadership or trustees. Again, this works better when the meeting is dedicated to this process to allow people time to ask questions, understand the report, and find a way to move forward aligning with the church culture. If you have hired a consultant for this process it might be hard for them to return to the church in person, particularly if they are out of state or some distance away. You will find that Skype or Zoom calls can work just as well. At the start of any engagement, factor this into your requirements when seeking proposals. If you want them to come on-site and present the findings of the report, tell them so, then factor this into the budget and ask them to call this out in their proposal.

Once the report is written it will lay bare the security deficiencies of your organization, which can be a concern for some. What happens if something goes wrong? Has this report increased our liability if we knew of an issue and didn't correct it? Here's the sad reality; you will be sued for not having a safety program and you will be sued if your program is inadequate. There is no "safe" in this world, only "safer". The reason why you started this process was to improve and make your church safer. The purpose of the meeting is to discuss what the church can do now. If you cannot afford a certain security measure, let the meeting minutes show this. If you need capital expense for a long-term technology strategy, again document this in the minutes and say when it must come back to the committee for review.

The expectation is not that you implement every single recommendation within the assessment report but prioritize and find those that work within your budget and culture of the church. Remember, whatever you do or don't do in security will always be challenged, but keep in mind you went into this process with good intentions. If something should ever go wrong, did you know about the fault?

Was there a plan? Even putting something off until you have time and money is a plan. Can you articulate why you made the decisions that you made? In our everyday lives, we prioritize things all the time, but if everything is a priority then nothing becomes a priority. The biggest challenge I see for many churches following the issuance of the report is finding the time to complete the actions. Receiving the report is only the start of the journey. Someone will need to hold individuals accountable when they have been assigned tasks to ensure the tasks get completed. Perhaps this is you?

Lastly, it is important to present the findings to the leaders of your church, not only to continue with the strong security culture but to ensure you have the buy-in on the direction you want to go as well as support for funding. One thing I have found is that security managers, facilities leaders, and administrators have been banging their heads against brick walls for years about security issues and no one listens or takes action. I walk in the door and make some suggestions and change tends to happen because I am an outsider and a perceived expert. Presenting the security assessment to a church leader who you feel will listen, who you have a good rapport with, and who has the background to legitimize what the report is saying will help the cause. We've all worked with nonprofits and know how much politics can play a part in decision making. Take your time, find the best person amongst church leadership, and give them the tools to be successful.

NOTES

STEP FIVE

—

Write Policy and Procedures

—

Therefore everyone who hears these words of Mine and acts on them, may be compared to a wise man who built his house on the rock. And the rain fell, and the floods came, and the winds blew and slammed against that house; and yet it did not fall, for it had been founded on the rock

MATTHEW 7:24-25

Up until this point, we have been focusing on building a solid foundation for your safety program. If you have followed the previous steps outlined in this book, you are already ahead of most other churches. The steps you have followed have established a stronger security culture and have given you ways that you can continue to improve over time. You are also better equipped to look at safety more holistically and are considering "all hazards" when protecting your perimeter and you have conducted a security assessment of your building and programs. So, what next? Documentation. Now that you have a plan, your processes must be documented. Why? Quite simply as in Matthew 7:24-25, we need a solid foundation for the house to stand up. How can you enforce the standard if you don't have a standard? How do you want people to respond or know what to do if you have not told them?

I had an opportunity to speak in front of a large group of church administrators. There were 60-70 different faith organizations present. During our conversation, I asked them to raise their hand if they had a formal policy and procedure document that they used to train and educate staff. Approximately 15-20 hands went up in the air. I then asked the group to keep their hand raised if they had all of their security procedures documented. Half of this group lowered their hands. Only a small group of administrators had performed this important step in the process. My point is that you are certainly not alone in this task. The fact you have taken the time to read this book shows that you are taking this seriously and really want to make a difference. So, don't be embarrassed to call a friend or a neighboring church for advice on policies and procedures, you may be surprised at how similar your situations are.

WHAT IS THE DIFFERENCE BETWEEN A POLICY AND A PROCEDURE?

A policy will make high-level statements such as "St Mary's Catholic Church will background check all volunteers working with children". The procedure will then go on to describe how this will be achieved i.e. (1) Each volunteer working with children will take a background check once per calendar year. (2) The person is required to provide their name, date of birth, and addresses of the last 7 years to the church administrator. (3) The volunteer manager will submit these to the local police department within five days. (4) The volunteer manager will review all criminal histories identified and assess if it affects the person's ability to work with children. Policy statements are rules to be followed and procedures explain how the rule is followed in a step by step guide.

PROCEDURES. WHERE DO YOU START?

A good place to start is to write down a list of scenarios of things that could happen at your church. I call these "when this happens statements". My good friend, security expert, and former Presidentially appointed US Marshal for Colorado, Tina Rowe, uses a similar phrase that I really like; "what could go wrong?" You are having a pool party with 10 kids and one adult. Several of the kids cannot swim. What could go wrong? Tina says that by asking ourselves what can go wrong in any given situation helps identify risk. Once we know our risks we can work on mitigation controls. In this case, what could go wrong? Well, if two or three of those young kids who cannot swim need help, one adult cannot help all of them, so, the "what can go wrong" has led us to the conclusion we need more supervision, or someone could drown.

If you have policies and procedures in place, find a date to review them. Get a group of people together who have a vested interest in the success of the program; finance officers, preschool workers, safety volunteers, and HR teams are a great place to start. These roles understand risk and will be important in providing you with constructive feedback. The review process does not always move along quickly and can be difficult at times, but the results will be worthwhile and rewarding. When I was at the MOA, we would conduct this review yearly, which is what I would highly recommend. The security leadership would convene to go through each governance document line by line. By doing this, it ensured we had the right information and that we knew our procedures in detail. As we reviewed each document we would ask these questions:

» What is the risk behind this policy/procedure?

» Does the policy/procedure still safeguard against the risk?

» What, if anything, needs to be changed?

» What is the justification for making a change?

» Will the change affect any other departments?

As one might imagine, this process took a tremendous amount of time, however, we were committed to the process because of how valuable it was to our operations. As you complete your review, remember to save your documents, and use some level of version control i.e. V.1 V.2 V.3, etc. as it's a great way to chart the evolvement of the processes, showing where you came from to where you intend to go. Should something ever go wrong, it's ideal to have documentation showing governance over your processes. Take it from me, saving the document and backing them up is key, and we learned that lesson the hard way when our scribe lost all of the work we had performed, and we had to repeat the process losing hours of work – ouch!

IF YOU DON'T HAVE GOVERNANCE DOCUMENTED, DON'T PANIC!

You are not the first and you will certainly not be the last! By conducting your security assessment (Step 4) and interviewing staff, volunteers, and members of your congregation you will have a good idea of the risks at your church. The steps in this book are designed to be completed in order but it's not uncommon for these steps to be completed out of sequence. If you have an existing program there might be verbal processes that people follow. So, if you haven't yet completed your security assessment and need to review your procedural processes, here's some guidance.

A few paragraphs back, I said to write down the "when this happens" or Tina Rowe's "what could go wrong" statements. Write some notes down as to what your current security response would be to these questions. It doesn't need to be detailed, just start the process. Here are a few examples:

» If/when a father comes in who has a no-contact order against his children, what is your response?

» Someone observes suspicious behavior?

» There is a medical emergency?

» A person starts shouting at your religious leader?

» A child goes missing?

» A couple arguing in your parking lot?

» You have a severe weather warning?

» You hear gunshots?

» You need to evacuate the building?

» Someone refuses a church background check, or the check comes back with a criminal history?

» Where does the offering go after collection?

» A new member at church wants to serve but has a history of crime in their background. What would you do in this situation?

» How do you handle someone disrupting a service?

» What would you do if someone brings alcohol or shows up drunk on your property?

» How do you handle trespassing?

There is no trick question. These are everyday things that you are likely to see in your church. Prioritize what is important, things like an active shooter incident happening at your church are rare but have a high impact. Start writing the most likely scenarios first as you will find lots of crossover in actions and responses. For example, if you tell people to shelter in place for severe weather, it is similar to the "hide" aspect of "run, hide, fight", in an active shooter situation. If you tell people to evacuate the building for a disturbance, this is similar to the "run" aspect. Run, Hide, Fight is broken down later in this step.

SOME EXAMPLES

There isn't a list that I can provide you with that has everything you will ever need as security is always evolving. The list below is a strong starting point of the procedures that you should have documented within your program.

Access Control - When are doors unlocked? Which doors are unlocked? What is the protocol for unlocking doors? How often are doors checked?

Aggressive Behavior - How should staff respond? At what point do you call the police? Who takes the lead?

Background Checks - ANYONE working with children then prioritize which staff and volunteers need background checks and how often. I would go back as far as the state law allows but then consider the following for review to hire regardless: 1) age of criminal act or civil wrong, 2) time since act committed, 3) contriteness, 4) what has the person done since? Backgrounds for both paid and volunteer positions should include calling former employers even if work was volunteering and conduct interviews by a skilled interviewer. Pull motor vehicle records if driving and financial check if working with money.

Building Evacuation - How is the building evacuated or searched? Who needs to be informed of a building evacuation?

Bomb Threat - Who should be informed? How do you determine if a threat is credible?

CCTV and Retention - How long is CCTV video stored? Who can access it and for what purposes? What is the process for releasing it to law enforcement or other requestors?

Custody Disputes - What proactive safety measures should be taken during a custody battle and non-contact orders? What happens if an altercation takes place on church property? What safeguards should be put in place to ensure children are kept safe?

Domestic Violence - Who and when should you call? What support is offered to a victim?

Incident Log - Even incidents that turn out to be nothing should be recorded. Whether it is suspicious behavior, an unauthorized access attempt to a room or area, theft, burglary, etc. There should be an incident log maintained of all safety and security incidents at the church to chart potential and actual security breaches.

Lockdown Procedure - How is the building secured? "Run, Hide, Fight" model.

Lost/Missing Child - Where should staff look first? What are the safety protocols in place? Who speaks with the child's parents? Who discusses the incident if the local or national media call? What happens if the child is not found after a few minutes?

Medical Emergency - What is the level of response? How and where do you find a first aider? What level of training do staff and volunteers need, is a medical certification required?

Money Movements - When and where is the offering money moved? What is the process for counting and banking the money?

Notification Tree - Who should be contacted in the event of a safety or security-related issue? How is this person contacted?

Severe Weather - Where do people go? Who can make the call on severe weather vs an emergency? Who calls the 'all clear'?

Suspicious Behavior - How do you handle suspicious incidents? Who should respond?

Suspicious Items - How do you clear an item with and without law enforcement support? How do you declare an item as safe?

Training Schedule - How often is emergency preparedness training conducted for staff? What are the mandatory trainings? What are the necessary certifications the team must have?

Training Records - How is training completed and recorded? How do you prove the training took place?

Unattended Items - What course of action should be taken for unattended items? What indicators are cause for escalation?

Use of Force - What are the available force options? When can these be used?

KEEP YOUR PROCEDURES LEAN!

When you are writing or reviewing your procedures, think of your audience at every step. How old are they? What are their backgrounds? What is their role and how critical is their position? The reason I say this is people often feel that procedures need to be long and detailed and this could lead to complications and confusion. When it comes to safety, the best advice I can give you is to write them as short, impactful statements that anyone can follow. Allow for flexibility where possible. Remember, these procedures will be followed under stressful conditions such as the Sandy Hook massacre we discussed in step 3. To protect themselves and the children, the schoolteachers had to lock a door which isn't so simple when you are under stress. You lose your fine motor skills and children's lives rest with your actions. So, it is important to provide the reader opportunity to adapt and deviate from the procedure when needed. You do not want them so fixated that they feel it should only occur a certain way. When the procedure is tested in real life, it just might not work the way you had planned, and this is very common. Remember your audience, remember the situation. During events like active shooter situations, stress levels will be high so the plan should not be too complicated. Keep it simple!

Another common question I get is how to handle a lost child situation. One example of a procedure for a lost child could be:

Find the person who last saw the child and ask them for a physical and clothing description and the area they were last seen- Search the area where the child was last seen.

1. If not found immediately summon help from others

2. If the child is not found within a reasonable amount of time (you determine this) call 911 and widen the search

3. Conduct a systematic search of the entire church campus

4. This is just an example of how straightforward you can make it. You might want to add more detail, but hopefully, you understand my point.

I wanted to break down the government's "run, hide, fight" guidance as it's another question I commonly get asked.

RUN MEANS

Step 1: Run away as fast as you can. Climb through windows or open doors to get away from the situation as quickly as possible

Step 2: Keep away, do not look back until you are far from the danger

Step 3: Call emergency services

Step 4: Do not return to the building unless instructed by emergency services

HIDE MEANS

Step 1: Go to a room where you cannot be seen, and you can lock the door

Step 2: Take other people with you if possible, but don't wait for them

Step 3: Turn your phone to silent and do not talk

Step 4: Stay in place until given the all-clear by someone in authority

FIGHT MEANS

Step 1: Fight or attack the offender like your life depends on it

Step 2: Use anything as a weapon such as chairs, stools, and other heavy items

Step 3: Fight as a group if able

Many people ask me about templates they find online. I'm not a fan of templates as I think everyone can create their own procedures. If you focus on what is important, not the style of the document, or how glossy it is, your procedure can become extremely effective. Remember, the main point is to inform your team and help them remember the steps. I see lots of churches cut and paste from documents they have been given or found online but this is about taking action, not just saying we have a document. Make sure you can train people to the standard you outline. Using other churches' response procedures are dangerous as each church is different.

MAKING CHANGES TO YOUR PROCEDURES

Keep in mind these documents will never be complete. There will always be a change, review, correction, or revision that needs to be made. What was good last week may no longer be the standard today. The recommendation is that the policies and procedures you have in place should be reviewed at least annually. Make sure to document your procedures and as I said earlier by keeping version controls. It prevents reinventing the wheel and you can capture your thought processes. Lastly, in a church, you might not always be in charge of the area you write the procedure for. When there is turnover, it helps a new person learn the history.

DEVELOPING AN EMERGENCY ACTION PLAN (EAP)

As you develop and grow your program, build your procedures into an Emergency Action Plan (EAP). An EAP is a document that outlines all your emergency procedures and what to do if one were to occur. Depending on the state you live in and organization size it can be a required document by Occupational Safety and Health Administration (OSHA).

At a basic level, the EAP should include:

- » A list of most common types of emergencies and critical resources for each type

- » A breakdown of the responsibilities of each emergency response team member during an incident

- » A flipchart of response actions that can be provided to teachers, church staff, and volunteers

» A communication call tree on who to notify during an emergency

TESTING YOUR PROCEDURES

A procedure is only as good as its effectiveness. How do you know it is effective if it's not being tested? Once written, you must test your procedures regularly starting with those most critical. This is what we would call assurance or compliance testing. There are several ways you can do this. One way is to attend staff meetings and ask questions so that people can show their competency in your plans. Another common way to test amongst security professionals is a process called "red teaming". It is a process to conduct a controlled test of a procedure looking for a desired outcome or response.

An example: your procedure says that the church custodian will walk around the building to check that all doors and windows are locked before they leave for the night. On a few occasions, members of staff have come to you saying they have found the ground floor windows open. You want to create a test to see if the custodian is following the procedure. You purposefully leave 2-3 windows open, then return to the building after the custodian has conducted their nightly rounds to see if they closed these windows. No matter the outcome, you tell the custodian that you have performed a test and notify them of the results. Another example would be to test a team member's response to suspicious activity. You place a person (actor) inside the church and tell them to act a certain way, knowing a member of staff will walk past and see them. You have a protocol in place for how to deal with breaking of social boundaries. How does the staff member respond? Do they follow procedures or keep walking? You declare the results as a test and debrief with them what they did well or highlight areas to improve. When creating a red teaming exercise, it's important to have the right mindset as to what the desired outcome is. You are checking that your processes work correctly. It might not be the person you are testing that is at fault if a process fails. Type up an overview with the goals, objectives, scenario description, and desired outcome. This makes the process transparent and fair.

Here's an example: the purpose of this red team exercise is to test the unattended item procedure. A box will be left inside the church against a pillar of the worship center. The box will have a small wire visible from the outside and will be sealed by tape. The objective is to see if team member X will spot the box, follow the training, and report the item as unusual.

HAVE A CONTROL MEASURE IN PLACE

Through red teaming, you may create a simulation that might cause a person to raise alarm by calling the police, escalating the situation to a senior leader, or evacuating the building. As Tina Rowe would say "you are about to test your unattended item policy, what can go wrong?" How do you stop a person calling the police or evacuating the building during one of your tests? You need to put a control measure in place that would stop this. Perhaps tell some key people what you are doing or watch the person on your security cameras. When they start to clear the area or take action, declare this a test. It could be that you invite your local crime prevention officer to come help, so they are onsite. We don't use our local police departments enough during training and procedure testing. Whatever it looks like for you, have a control in place that would prevent the person from calling 911 if it wasn't a real emergency.

DISCUSS RED TEAM RESULTS

When you have concluded the test, tell the person it was a test and in a private room talk them through the objective and what the desired outcome was. Did they pass or fail? No one likes to be singled out or receive feedback if they 'failed'. This is the sensitive part of the test. The goal is for you both to learn, improve, and move forward. This is not an "a-ha, we got" you moment. We've all made mistakes, had errors of judgment, been tired, or distracted. Remember quite often it's the procedure that doesn't work not the person following it. This exercise is about learning what goes on "off paper". Record the results so you have captured the history of the test. If the person failed, wait a few days or weeks and test that same person again. It will allow them to use the training or refresher you have provided and bring back their self-confidence when they pass. If they failed again really work to understand why. Was it a systemic issue that would have happened to any staff or volunteer member? Find the root cause and when you discover it, don't stop there as a new gap has been identified. How are you going to correct it? Who do you need to discuss this with? What action needs to be taken?

When you get success stories, or when someone 'passes', make sure you share these as well. It tells your leadership to have confidence in your program, progress is being made, and boosts the confidence of staff and volunteers. Your safety committee is a good group to share how many red team exercises you have completed and what the results were.

NOTES

....

....

....

....

....

....

....

....

....

....

STEP SIX

—

Conduct Safety Training

—

Give instruction to a wise man and he will be still wiser, teach a righteous man and he will increase his learning

PROVERBS 9:9

TRAIN, TRAIN, AND TRAIN SOME MORE!

No matter what industry you are in, the number one asset for any business is their people. This is no different in a church, especially when we are looking at creating a safer environment. As I mentioned in Step 3, security is a layered approach, having several layers of protection working together against a specific threat. All staff and volunteers in your house of worship should be trained in some capacity to know how to protect your church from people wanting to cause your community harm.

When looking at who should be trained, start with people in critical positions that have the biggest exposure to risk (children/money/outreach programs etc.) As previously mentioned, Carl Chinn of the Faith-Based Security Network published statistics about deadly force incidents in houses of worship. The statistics show that most acts of deadly force occur during the week, not just during Sunday services as we might assume, so we must train our people to be ready at all times. A critical position is any role that interacts with the public and could help identify suspicious behaviors or take action when something goes wrong. Each house of worship is different, but when you consider what could be a critical role, it can be broad. Here are a few examples:

» Facilities Staff

» Front Desk

» Ushers/Greeters

» Preschool/Youth Ministry

» Ministry Teams

» Safety Teams

» Medical Teams

TRAINING MUST REFLECT THE RISKS

Training staff and volunteers should always reflect the risks of your organization such as deadly force, medical emergencies, weather hazards, and child safety. A common list of training for houses of worship should include:

» Security procedures (Lost child, parent non-contact order, etc.)

» Situational awareness

» Suspicious behavior training

» Conversational interviewing

» Verbal de-escalation

» Scenario training

» Evacuation (Lockdown, fire, bomb threat)

» Severe weather

» Dealing with mental illness/chemical and alcohol dependency

» Medical emergencies

» Firearms

THE MOST BENEFICIAL TRAINING, SUSPICIOUS BEHAVIOR!

Since the tragic events of 9/11, the government has used the slogan "see something say something", but this can be difficult when a church is supposed to be based on community and fellowship. It's one of the biggest challenges in security ministry. There can be a stigma that by raising the alarm or identifying people as 'different', we are not being true to our faith. In fact, you find it's the opposite. Seeing unusual behavior is often an opportunity to minister to those in need.

Violence and crime can often be prevented by addressing the unusual behaviors before they escalate to the point of action. These behaviors are generally signs of deeper problems. Addressing them early allows us to diffuse what could be a potentially harmful or criminal situation. It's important to remember that situations displaying suspicious behavior are not necessarily a precursor for a criminal act, nor are they indicators of actual risk. They help guide us to recognize risk factors and determine what action to take.

When you think of recent mass murderers, the offenders have

all displayed behaviors that signaled their intent before they committed their crimes, but remember suspicious behavior is not exclusive to deadly force. It could be that they are looking to steal from the church or abduct their child that they are no longer permitted to see. There are always signs that things are not well. In raising your situational awareness and being educated on what to look out for, we can increase our guardianship and keep our church communities safe. The challenge becomes, how do we identify the "see something" in a church where all people are welcome, and everyone is the same in the eyes of the Lord? As a Christian and former English detective, I have used my police experience to educate churches on four rules that allow Christ followers to tackle this difficult subject and do so from a position of grace. I personally consider situational awareness and the ability to spot suspicious behavior in your church as the backbone of your whole church safety program where everyone can play their part. To that end, I am going to go into detail of four rules that I have developed to help keep people safe.

The first rule is that suspicious behavior does not mean that something is wrong. One Sunday, I walked into a church and saw a large suitcase outside a men's restroom. My mind started racing, I thought of all the things it could be as it looked out of place. "Evacuate the area" "call the police" were some of the things that crossed my mind, but as I walked into the restroom, I found out that one of the foreign ministry leaders who was going on a mission trip had simply left his suitcase outside. It was a lesson for me. It's important to remember that society is still full of good people and yes we must be cautious in our environment, but most of what you see and consider suspicious will likely have a reasonable explanation. "Trust but verify" can be an excellent guiding principle when encountering suspicious activity.

The second rule of suspicious behavior is that it starts with the breaking of a social boundary. In the church, asking people to identify suspicious behavior sometimes has a negative stigma attached to it. It can give off the impression that you are not very welcoming or are casting judgment over someone's appearance or social status, but when I ask people to look for the breaking of a social boundary, they seem to find it easier to contextualize. I was at church one Sunday when a woman entered the sanctuary holding a jewelry box. I watched as she stood in front of the pastor moments before he was about to start his sermon. Everyone else was sat down. Almost immediately she started shouting and threw the jewelry box up in the air. My attention was drawn to her, not because of her appearance, but the fact she broke a social boundary. Standing in front of the pastor right before he was going to start his sermon was not something you normally see at my church. You know your church environment better than anyone and when you see the breaking of a social boundary, it can lead to an act of suspicious behavior.

The third rule is that suspicious behavior can be detected through the worship attack cycle. The worship attack cycle is a series of behaviors that are often completed before a criminal act takes place. It shares the same principles as the terrorist planning cycle. First, the offender will identify your church as a target. Once they have done this, they will start to research your church and collect information about program activities, often online and through social media. Information that they cannot find online will force them to come to your church and observe worship. Once they know your environment, they plan their criminal act. When they are ready, they will come back and practice until they feel comfortable taking action.

It's important you know the role you play in disrupting the worship attack cycle. At the observe worship and practice phases, you can interrupt those motivated offenders by spotting their breaking of social boundaries as the offender will physically be at the church during these phases. They can complete the other phases at home when they are online but to conduct surveillance and to practice, they need to physically come inside your church.

The behaviors to look for at the observation stage are people wandering without a purpose, asking unusual questions, being found in restricted areas, people in the church for an extended period, and breaking social boundaries. You may also see other out of place behaviors that include not wearing appropriate clothing for the season or deliberately leaving items unattended. It's important to remember rule number one. Suspicious behavior does not mean that something is wrong, but recognizing it is our chance to make sure everyone is ok and minister those in need.

The 4th rule is often the most important; trust your instinct for things that look out of place. During the Boston Marathon bombing, then 21-year-old Jeff Bauman was waiting for his girlfriend to cross the finish line when he was severely injured during the explosion. At the hospital, he told FBI agents that he knew who was responsible for the attack and he was right! He explained that he had seen those responsible at the finish line and that they didn't look right. They had no interest in the race, they faced away from the finish line when everyone else was cheering, they were seen carrying heavy backpacks, and had blank facial expressions. Bauman said that contextually they just didn't fit with the other people at the finish line.

Have you ever been traveling in a car when you've had a near-miss of an accident? Your hands start to sweat, your heart beats faster, and you feel a rush of blood to the head. You know your body is telling you, "that was a close call" and for the next two minutes you slow down to recover from the rush of emotion. I believe that God gave you those instincts so you can spot danger and keep safe, but we often fear these instincts in a church setting through fear of judgment. You may think "what if I am wrong?" We can't live in fear, and it's important to learn through the experiences of others. You know what your gut is telling you, God gave you those instincts. Trust them and know they came to you for a reason.

Remember, those displaying suspicious behavior could be the very people that you are wanting to serve and need your help the most. I know what I am asking you to do is hard, but being proactive, and using these four rules as a guide will help keep you and your ministry safe!

No matter what your role is in the church, I believe that all criminal activity you see will have started with some type of suspicious behavior which is why it's important to know these four rules.

FINDING THE BEST WAY TO EDUCATE

In the last three to five years more and more of my training content has been pushed to OnDemand video learning at the Worship Security Association (WSA). One of the reasons for this is that in today's world not everyone has the time to go to a church for training. What I noticed was that churches would hire me to talk and people couldn't attend due to personal commitments or simply the time it was held didn't work for them. I had the idea to create a video platform that staff and volunteers could watch anytime, anywhere, streamed at home or together at the church.

Go take a look at worshipsecurity.org

WSA allows churches to subscribe to the ever-growing video library and use it to train staff and volunteers, but not everyone responds to this style of teaching and that is ok. I have some churches that want me to come in person to present, and some just want me to come and hold discussions with their safety teams in a Q&A style format. My point here is do not be fixed on a certain style of training. People learn differently. Before you hire a safety professional to come and train, canvas the views of the prospective students and find out how they learn best. One of the reasons why WSA is so popular is that like me, many people in churches need time for the information to sink in. I will need to hear a training principle 2-3 times before it sinks in and I hate taking tests! Streaming videos on the WSA platform allows people the chance to watch the training multiple times at their own pace and the church doesn't have to worry about sustainment training or cost. In the previous section, I provided a list of areas that you need to train on as a church. What you need to do next is make sure you have the right methods on how you will train on each topic.

A key point to address first is who should conduct your training. There are several answers here, but finding someone qualified in the field, experienced, who understands the heart of your church, is insured and competent are crucial starting points. A lot of this depends on your budget. By asking your local law enforcement, members of your congregation, or by searching the internet, you will receive many recommendations. Just because someone is highly recommended doesn't mean you have to go forward with them. Remember are they (1) qualified (2) experienced (3) a good cultural fit with your church (4) insured. Talk with references and find out what other people think about them. I know most small churches do not have room in the budget when it comes to training, so your local police department is a great resource. Tap into your community. If you ask, I suspect you will find people that have many transferable skills and can help. Off duty law enforcement officers and safety professionals attend churches across the country, ask and find out where they are.

MAINTAIN TRAINING RECORDS

Maintaining records will provide you with a data source that can be used to defend your program against a challenge, assess the performance of your team, and track progress. When determining how long you should keep training records on file, you should refer to your church records retention policy. If your church does not have a policy, best practice would be to keep all records for five years. Keep track of all data sources, online training, continuing education, and in person training. You never know when your records will be needed.

In security ministry, we are often grateful just to have someone who will give their time and volunteer, but security is different than all other positions in the church. It is a highly-skilled role where extreme judgment calls must be made. As well as maintaining training records, set a standard of skill requirements that you want your teams to uphold. Working with volunteers is hard as we all have limited time, but this is one area of your ministry where you must enforce a standard. Without this, it can increase your liability. Jesus chose his disciples, he didn't take just anyone, he carefully selected each one of them and you should do the same. Make sure you have the right people overseeing the church's reputation.

PUBLISH A SCHEDULE WELL IN ADVANCE

One issue I hear about when working with safety team leaders is the lack of attendance at training. On the other hand, when talking with team members who are "doing the work" they tell me about the issues they face. "I couldn't make the training as we only got notified last week" or "I couldn't make my shift last Sunday as the schedule came out a few days before and I already had a family commitment". Does this sound familiar? A common struggle that perhaps you've heard before, so we must find the middle ground between leaders and team members. Create a training schedule well in advance to gain respect and buy-in from your team. The important aspect is giving volunteers the time to move their personal life around their commitment to serve.

My experience has told me it's almost impossible to get all your team together for training without someone missing it. The best thing you can do is set a firm date and don't move it around based on everyone else's other commitments. Create a calendar that you can publish and if you can, offer the same training twice. I have a couple of jobs and a young family, but love helping with security ministry and other serving opportunities at my church, so I need to plan my calendar in advance. Here's a simple guide to help you:

» Determine the areas that you want to train on

» Set the dates for the next 6-12 months, let your teams know

» If people cannot make the dates proceed anyway, don't change them

» If people don't attend regularly, meet them one on one and ask why. Hold them accountable for the volunteer commitment they made

GIVE SOMEONE THE ROLE OF TRAINER

Find someone on your team who performs well, has the heart of a teacher, and can carry out the role of safety trainer. This role has a dual purpose; they oversee the continuous monitoring of your training and handle the intake of new safety volunteers to ensure that everyone is trained consistently before they can work on your team. This helps with training on key areas such as the use of the radio, church policies, protocols, and making your onboarding process more effective. If you don't already do onboarding, this is a good time to start. You can also use this role for red team drills to check that procedures are understood and followed. They can either support the red teaming of your safety team or support the development of those that fail. Have a person in charge of your training to remove the burden from a church administrator, facilities manager, or church volunteer who is likely already over-burdened with responsibility.

CONDUCT TABLETOP EXERCISES

Tabletop exercises are a fantastic way to learn as a group. These can be as simple as inviting your safety team or church leadership to walk through a scenario and modifying it as you grow, develop, and improve. There can be a hesitation with tabletop exercises as they are not the "real thing" but they are a great way to check and challenge decisions should an incident occur in real-time. Walking through an active shooter scenario has a very different feel to it as opposed to the actual event happening but outlining what to do in these high-stress incidents will pay off as it builds muscle memory and confidence. The average active shooter in-cident lasts less than six minutes according to the Department of Homeland Security statistics. Making wrong decisions or not making any decisions at all can be costly. My good friend Joe Bezotte who is a Special Agent and Use of Force Instructor with his company Core Security Consulting introduced me to a saying "the body cannot go where the mind hasn't been". Tabletops are a good way to prepare the mind for that day when evil comes. You don't need to overthink a tabletop exercise. Come up with a scenario that is most likely to happen at your church, get the core people together, and walk through the process. There are many templates online that you can use to help to get started.

NOTES

. . . .

. . . .

. . . .

. . . .

. . . .

. . . .

. . . .

. . . .

. . . .

. . . .

. . . .

. . . .

. . . .

. . . .

. . . .

STEP SEVEN

—

Start a Safety Team

—

And Jesus entered the temple and drove out all those who were buying and selling in the temple, and overturned the tables of the money changers and the seats of those who were selling doves. And He said to them, "It is written, 'My house shall be called a house of prayer'"

MATTHEW 21:12-13

This verse illustrates one of the few times in scripture that we see Jesus' frustration as His Father's house of prayer was being taken over by those selling goods. He forcibly drives them out and shows his anger by overturning tables inside the temple. How can this story relate to establishing a safety team? As Jesus said, my Father's house shall be called a house of prayer, but history has shown this is not always the case. There are people in our houses (in our case, churches) that come to cause us harm as they do not see it as a house of prayer. When human brokenness enters our churches, we need a pre-planned response, a safety team, to take action should this brokenness lead to criminal behavior.

I was talking with a friend Jim Howard who lives in Florida. Jim runs an organization called Trinity Security Allies, a nonprofit focused on biblical security ministry. He has also spent many years consulting with churches on safety. He said something that struck me, and it made me think about why we need safety teams. He said "Simon, there are three reasons people go to church. (1) They believe in the Lord our savior and are happy and at peace with their lives (2) they are hurting, feeling some type of pain and need the sanctuary of the Lord to guide them (3) they are a wolf in sheep's clothing pretending to be number 1 and 2 so they can cause us harm". We need a safety team with a pre-planned response for those wolves in sheep's clothing as well as to help support those hurting and in pain. In today's world, there is so much human brokenness, mental illness, and crime that houses of worship are no longer the safe havens they once were. To the motivated offender, they are an establishment with an open-door policy, soft targets, and easy pickings.

We need a safety team to ensure that legal and moral obligations are met to keep the church community safe and have a pre-planned response to emergency situations. If you are struggling to find support at this stage, remember to utilize your safety committee and seek their support to influence change and create a culture where security is nurtured.

Here's a scenario I give people struggling with the justification of starting a team. You want to host a concert in your local park one Sunday afternoon and hire in a well-known band. You hope to have around 400 people attend and there will be loud music and refreshments. What do you expect the city to say? Sure, come on down do what you want, invite who you want, sell your tickets far and wide. No, we know the answer. Do you have permits? Do you have a safety plan? Who will do traffic control? You'll need approval from the Fire Marshall.... the list will go on and on, but would you be surprised? No. Why? Because you are a place of mass gathering where you have a responsibility to those around you.

I teach a class called "Safety in Places of Worship". I mentioned a parable earlier when Jesus is tested by the Pharisees in Luke

20:21. This parable helps us demonstrate our responsibility to both God and country. The Pharisees were trying to trap Jesus into declaring that it was ok to pay taxes to Caesar. If He did so, He would be saying that there is someone higher than God. Scripture tells us many times that God should come before all things.

Caesar was the ruler of the land and there was a legal obligation to pay taxes. This is no different to where we are today. The law of the land (Caesar) is that we must provide a safe environment. We are governed by many laws from the Occupational Safety and Health Administration (OSHA) to employment laws where we need to adhere to specific codes regarding how we construct our churches and homes. These laws must be followed no matter your religious beliefs.

The simple fact of the matter is that in security ministry we should put God before all things. We also have a legal and moral obligation to ensure that people within our faith communities are kept safe. Having a safety team is about having a pre-planned response and fulfilling our legal obligation. We should never forget that when the day of evil comes to our houses of worship, we will be tested by the law on the adequacy of our safety program. Give to Caesar what is Caesars (appropriate protection required by law) and give to God what is God's (protection of ALL his people). Why I like to use this piece of scripture is not only because of how Jesus handles the situation, but how relevant His response is today in correlation as to why you need a safety team.

As we get started in this chapter, I want to address something that should not be overlooked. Last year I held a church firearms awareness class at a police gun range with my friend Virginia (Ginny) Cronin who is a nonprofit attorney for Henningson & Snoxell. One of the first things that the gun range asked for was a copy of my general liability insurance. In today's world, everyone has (or should I say needs) coverage. I provided the range with a copy of my certificate then called my insurance broker, Bullis Insurance, to seek advice and make sure I had the right coverage in place for this public event. Although you should seek advice from your insurer at all stages of your safety program, I mention it here because with a team of volunteers, your liability increases. What if they get injured in this role? What happens if they injure someone else? Calling your insurance agent before starting a safety team will allow you to explain to them that you are looking to create a safety team and check you have the right coverage, learn what you are covered for, and to seek advice. They have been asked these types of questions hundreds of times and can offer you sound advice.

Something else that I recommend that you do is seek advice from a nonprofit attorney like my friend Ginny. If you don't have an attorney, seek out someone in your faith community that might support you pro bono or has prior knowledge of a good one. Even as a consultant I repeatedly ask Ginny for advice from someone who knows the law. Do you understand all the legal implications of having a safety team? Do the people that will join the team know and understand their rights? Speaking with an insurance agent and attorney are the two things I would do today to make sure you know you're on the right path.

WE'RE BACK TO UNDERSTANDING CULTURE AGAIN!

Later on in this chapter, we will cover some of this in more detail but whether you are a church leader and have asked someone to create a safety team or you are a concerned member of your congregation approaching your religious leader on the subject, you will need to do something first. Go back to Step 1 and understand your security culture. I would even replace "culture" this time with the word "mission". What is your mission? There are many questions to be asked to understand your church's appetite before you even start to move forward. Some of the questions to seek answers to are:

» Has the church spoken to their insurers on this subject, what advice did they give?

» Have you sought to better understand the legal implications of having a safety team before you start planning?

» Who will the safety team consist of? Employees or church volunteers?

» What equipment do you wish for your safety team to have? Firearms, baton, no defensive weapon, or only verbal de-escalation? All of the above are OK, it boils down to your church's culture!

» Has the church leadership blessed the creation of this team? Are they aware?

» Has the security ministry been given the same status as outreach programs and foreign ministry? Remember if people do not feel safe they do not come to church, if they do not come to church, the offering goes down, if the offering goes down then the church cannot do outreach, if the church cannot do outreach, then it cannot do ministry work. We need to be recognized as a ministry just like any other ministry in the church.

» Is there a budget assigned and what is the approval process?

There are many other things I could list here, these are just examples. You should sit down together before you even start to work on a format and understand the culture and mission around some of these questions. It will set you up for success as you move forward.

SOME THOUGHTS ON BUDGET

I have worked with churches long enough to know that if you are a small church, you are more than likely investing in this program yourself which means that you don't have much money to spend. If you are a medium or large church you are more than likely working with a reduced or nonexistent budget. If you are not one of these, you are in a blessed position and I know that you are appreciative. I know that funding is short across most churches. Many times, people are paying for security measures themselves, and nine times out of ten the appropriate budget has not been set. I want to give you a few tips of things that you can do on limited resources.

If you are not the holder of the church budget I suggest sitting with the person who is. Provide them a short business case in a PowerPoint slide deck or Word document laying out what you think you need, why you need it, and what it may cost. You need to show that you are taking this seriously and for them to understand that this isn't going away. Before you hold this conversation, bench-mark with other churches in your area. At this stage, you are specifically looking for those churches around you that have safety teams so you can ask questions about funding, budget, and how they got started. No two churches are the same. It comes down to two words I've mentioned before: "culture" and "environment".

Look for ways to share costs with different ministries. For example, who is currently paying for the background checks for staff and volunteers? Can you collaborate with other ministries to pool resources? What can be donated? Safety is not always about money. Can someone give you advice and support pro bono or donate equipment that you might need? Either way, you should create a formal budget as to what you feel the next one to four years might look like.

WHO WILL LEAD THE TEAM?

If this is not you and you are a leader at your church looking for the right person to lead a safety team, here is my advice - put someone in charge!

High-profile startup companies are generally started by entrepreneurs without job titles. "We're all at the same level here" you hear the leaders say. These young executives and innovators sit around on bean bag chairs working flexible hours to enhance creativity and production; however, you don't hear of these stories much anymore. Why? As they grow they realize that goals are unachievable this way. There is too much ambiguity and lack of structure that can prevent their company from growing and succeeding. I see it all too commonly in church safety programs. I went to a school recently to conduct a security assessment and asked who was in charge of security during a meeting. Four executives in the room raised their hands. When I asked who can I serve a subpoena for an impending lawsuit, they all lowered their hands and said it wasn't them. That isn't a part of the job that anyone likes, but you must have a clear leader and team structure. This can be a paid member of staff or volunteer, but ideally, it's someone who has the stature, respect, authority, and title to take action. They know they are in charge of safety within the organization and the organization recognizes this authority. Can you name this leader at your organization?

In my working life, I have built many teams and programs, reinvented the wheel a few times, and experienced all the difficulties that go along with managing people. Outside of parenting, managing people is one of the hardest jobs you can ever have in my opinion. One strength in management is recognizing that all the people on your team possess different skills and attributes – this runs parallel with running a safety program. If you already have a safety team in place, you should be asking "Do I have the right person?" If the answer is yes, continue to move forward. If there is doubt take a moment, reflect, and make a decision as to what your next steps are. There is a vast difference between asking someone to lead your existing team versus starting from scratch with a blank canvas. Depending on where you are at in this step it could be two different people. Whatever direction you take, it is about finding the "best person". Perhaps you even wait a month or two for the best person to become available if needs be.

Building something new requires patience, perseverance, being comfortable with ambiguity, change, a dynamic environment, and outside the box thinking. I often say to people that security ministry is not about being the most "called" but the most "capable".

A good friend of mine Wes Pederson is the Safety and Security Director at Eagle Brook Church here in Minnesota. They have nine campuses and depending on how you look at the numbers, they are the sixth-largest church in the country. This could be argued, but you get my point that they are big. Wes will be the first to tell you that he does not have a background in security, is not an expert in safety, and perhaps is not qualified for the position on paper. I disagree with him; he spent many years in the corporate world before entering into ministry. He is calm, composed, engaging, and a great leader. He knows the culture of Eagle Brook well and has surrounded himself with a core group of people he calls his "advisory team" of security experts. For some, his appointment as a security leader might have been unconventional, but it came down to the requirements of the church. What Eagle Brook needed was a composed leader who understood their culture to drive their safety programs forward and on many occasions, I go to him for advice on security ministry. The point I'm making is that the church's requirements drove the selection process, not the person feeling most called to do so. Security ministry is different than pretty much all other ministries you could list.

A couple of tips on how to find the best person. Remember, at Eagle Brook they wrote down their requirements as to what they needed, and my friend Wes matched the requirements. You know what you are looking for, so seek out those that would be a good fit. These could be police officers, military personnel, or people who work in security. A word of caution; unless they are in crime prevention roles, most police officers have a reactive security mindset. You should be seeking out someone with a proactive security mindset who is used to stopping the risk before it becomes a problem.

Even for a volunteer position, it's not uncommon to have a series of interviews, background checks, and discussions. Anyone with common sense knows that this is a difficult position to fill not just because it may be new in the church but because of the time commitment, training, writing, and program implementation. Perhaps you have a name in mind already as to who this person could be. I would urge you to take your time and find the right person especially if you are just starting. I've built several compliance and risk programs at two of the country's top financial institutions and I can tell you to be successful it takes time, dedication, and above all else selecting the right people.

I always like any person in safety and security to be members of the church. The reason why is because this role is different than ushers, greeters, and serving teams. They will need to train regularly to handle issues such as a domestic dispute, a lost child, or even a deadly force incident at your church. Your leader's actions also reflect your faith community. If they get it wrong and someone perceives they handled a situation poorly, then that could affect your church reputation. If they are required to take physical action they could hurt someone or themselves which could lead to a lawsuit. Having safety personnel that are members does not mitigate any of these events from occurring, but when they are called to act, you know that they have your best interests at heart. They have committed to your church, have a vested interest, and have the right motivations in serving. This can be hard depending on your faith community, but I would strongly encourage you to consider if your safety team should show their dedication to the church before they are allowed to serve.

CREATING TEAM RESPONSIBILITIES

When you have a leader in place you must decide on what your organization will look like. Remember my earlier example about these young fast-growing companies where no one had a role or job description, well now is the time you must determine one. You need this structure to set the team up for success!

Lay out the organizational chart and decide what your safety team will do. Start with the responsibilities first. It's not uncommon for larger churches to separate medical response from those acting in a safety capacity, but this is your opportunity to determine how it should look. Will ushers and greeters and other church programs be included, or will the safety team take the primacy and let them fulfill their own missions? Assigning leadership is biblically-based. In Exodus 18:21-23 Moses' father in law, Jethro, came to him to set up different levels of leadership to keep him focused and prevent him from wearing out. The same applies to a safety team wherein a leadership hierarchy is a must. It will remove stress from the director to help the team accomplish goals.

There is a fantastic local church that I work with who decided that they wanted to invest in their staff, so their entire safety team was made up of staff members. They have the stability and accountability that I mentioned earlier. Whatever this looks like for your faith community, make a decision, and get something implemented.

As an example, the common groups that make up most safety programs for Sunday worship is:

» Ushers and Greeters

» Safety/Security Team

» Medical Response Team

» Parking Team

» Ministry Teams

It is important to ensure that all those operating in the "first line of defense" are working together to reduce harm and mitigate risk.

HOW MANY PEOPLE DO I NEED?

One of the common questions people ask me is how big their church safety team should be. I know some teams that have four, five, or six people and others that have 40. It is a challenging question as many factors contribute to the size of your safety team:

» How many highly trained individuals can you get to join your team?

» Are all the entrances at your church covered by people that understand the security mindset? Do they have the confidence to raise the alarm if they see a red flag in someone's behavior or become concerned with a suspicious item?

» How many services do you have at your church?

» What would it take to have a supervisor, someone permanently inside your worship center, people at the doors conducting observations, and safety team members patrolling the area?

» Do you want the same volunteers at each service?

James McGarvey is the Executive Director of the Church Safety Guys and host of one of the largest church safety groups on Facebook with over 3,000 members. He told me that the research from his group suggests that most safety teams consist of 5-8% of their attendance size per service. This may help give you an idea of how big your safety team should be based on the size of your church. No matter the size of your church, if you can get five or six highly-trained safety team members that have good communication skills and understand their role, you will already be stronger than many other open-door environments.

Remember, the danger has to enter through one of your doors. Utilizing the greeters and parking lot volunteers will provide you with a safer environment knowing that if harmful intent or breaking of social boundaries occurs, you have the people who are confident to raise the alarm.

SELECTING THE RIGHT PEOPLE!
Luke 5:8-11

[8] But when Simon Peter saw that, he fell down at Jesus' feet, saying, "Go away from me Lord, for I am a sinful man!" [9] For amazement had seized him and all his companions because of the catch of fish which they had taken; [10] and so also were James and John, sons of Zebedee, who were partners with Simon. And Jesus said to Simon, "Do not fear, from now on you will be catching men." [11] When they had brought their boats to land, they left everything and followed Him."

It is important at the beginning and throughout the growth of your program that you use "The Jesus Approach". Jesus chose his disciples; he did not take recommendations. He didn't choose the ones that came forward. He selected each of them for a specific reason as it's incredibly important to find those that not only feel called, but those that bring forward the appropriate gifts such as compassion, communication, self-awareness, dedication, and available time. It's not uncommon that once you say you are starting a security ministry that people put themselves forward, often with good intentions, but they might not always be the right people. Remember these people play a key role within your ministry. You need the right personality traits that encompass the attitude and compassion for those that you serve.

You should proceed with caution to those that come saying "I know how to handle a gun, I was ex-military, ex-law enforcement or a permit to carry holder". Security ministry is about serving your church community. These people are a good fit only if they can display effective listening, effective verbal de-escalation, and can pray over people. They are far more likely to be helping those with human brokenness or a medical situation as opposed to running through your hallway like a swat team hunting down an active shooter. I accept that these skills are needed, but this is the exception, not the norm. If you don't think they can pray over someone in your community or sit with someone who has a mental illness for hours until professional services arrive, then you should think long and hard on their offer to join your security ministry.

I've found many fantastic retired police officers, security workers, and community leaders that want to get involved, but are past the age to practice unarmed physical tactics. They definitely can play an essential role on the team, just not from a physical standpoint.

I started to work with a church a few years ago where they had a 75-year-old retired chief of police on the team. His mind was extremely sharp, but when they hired a physical tactics person to come in, he would excuse himself. It was at this point that I started to tell churches to create a level approach to their safety teams. It was important to make sure they had a well-rounded team and played to people's strengths. That 75-year-old could observe and report and didn't need to walk around the building or worry about physical tactics. I have no doubt he could still spot the breaking of social boundaries when he becomes 100 years old. So how did I advise the church in their current status? We created a tiered approach.

Level 1 - Safety team (firearms trained)

Level 2 - Safety team unarmed

Level 3 - Behavior detection (observe and report for level 1&2)

Creating a leveled program allows you to define your training and standards for each role and then use people with the appropriate skills making sure (like all other areas of worship) you have an inclusive program. This 75-year-old had so much to offer but didn't want to carry a firearm or take on additional training, so level 3 was perfect for him! You can create standards for each level. Keep in mind there are always plenty of activities that an individual can do even if they aren't in top physical shape, have a physical handicap, or age is a concern (young or old). A greeter at any age can stand by the door and be the eyes and ears of the facility, as long as they have the skill set and passion to serve. The younger generation who are interested in law enforcement could be an excellent addition as it's important to train up the next generation.

We touched on this earlier, but the other factor on the selection process that I would strongly ask you to consider before you approach someone to be on your safety team is if they are a church member. What is a reasonable amount of time for them to have attended your faith community before they can serve?

I know of some churches that have taken people onto their safety team within weeks and months of them attending. I advise against this; they may have fantastic skills, but do you know enough about them? Are they committed to your faith community and protecting the flock? I serve in two areas at my church. I'm an advisor for our security ministry and help out on a four-week Life Transformed class where people learn to live like Jesus. I have done both of these for many years and they take up a lot of my time, but it shows the sustained commitment to my church.

Some facilities and administrators have gone even further and required that these people be Baptized by the church. Requesting that people on the team be members, perhaps Baptized, and committed is a fantastic way to ensure retention. They are volunteers after all, but the level of commitment needed here is far greater than any other ministry team you have. The church's reputation and safety can be at risk.

WHO ARE THE GOOD PEOPLE?

There is a tendency to fall into the comfort zone of taking on ex-military, police officers, and those with a permit to carry within your safety team. I fully support these people within your team for several reasons. They have had hours and hours of training in many areas from firearms to de-escalation. They have first-hand experience of confrontational and highly charged situations where decisions have to be made quickly and with precision, as people's lives and personal safety count on them. What I encourage you to do is create a team that is diverse and well rounded. Remember I cannot stress enough that most of what this team will do will be customer service and ministry-related, which relies on strong communication, empathy, and compassion.

What I have found is that having a diverse group of men and women with a security background, customer service, and an understanding of the mission of your faith community sets you up for success. You'll find that those with security backgrounds can help educate your ministries on awareness of risk and those with backgrounds in sales or community outreach often provide the platform of strong communication and service that allows your team to be balanced and successful.

When I joined the police in 1998, the background of those officers was not very diverse. When I look at my class photo, 98% of the officers were white males. A lot has changed over the years with a drive to make the police force more diverse to reflect the community that it serves, and I would echo this in security ministry. Aim for a team that represents the community that you serve. Women and people of different ethnic backgrounds should be included. In doing this everyone will bring a different skill set to the table. A word of warning; don't let the drive for diversity overshadow your requirements. The requirements should always come first as if a harmful or difficult situation does arise, you will need to know that the people you have selected can respond appropriately.

Some churches have safety team members fill out application forms. I do not have a strong opinion on this either way. I would say create a process of validation and corroboration. Do people within your faith community know these individuals? What are the personal views of their character? Can their background and experience be corroborated? If you need to follow a corporate process to do this then you should. A person should not expect to be hired on an application alone. I can't recall a single job where I haven't had some type of interview. Even if it's over a coffee in the church, you should ask some of the "what if" questions. This will help you understand firsthand their true character and allow you to make a decision. Be prepared; your answer in security ministry might not always be yes. A leader is most often judged on their "no's". You should prepare for a time when you have to say no!

A WORD ON BACKGROUND CHECKS

In a former life, I would interview employees who were suspected of money laundering. When interviewing employees and drawing up my conclusions, I cannot tell you how many times managers would ask for an exception to the rule for a mistake they said their employee might have made when handling money. Why is this story relevant to the backgrounds of your volunteers? Don't change your standards to suit the individual I had to say the process was the same for everyone no matter what their position. This should be the same for background checks. Do the same background checks for everyone. Every person on your team should have a comprehensive background check going back five to seven years. This should include all states and in the case of someone like me (a Brit living in America) should be covered internationally. Never change or deviate from your standards, as when you do Murphy's Law states this will be one time you get caught out.

This could include understanding their medical history and interviewing friends and family. If your safety team is going to be in a position where they might touch money, this could include a comprehensive financial check. There are many background checks out there ranging from $10 to $150 per check. Let me just remind you that you get what you pay for. It's ok to go the $10 route, but if something is missed you'll wish that you hadn't gone the cheap route and it will be too late. Taking this option is a risk in itself.

Create a process as to what is acceptable. If it comes back with a driving while intoxicated (DWI) from last year, is this ok? If the person is now 35 and when they were 20 they had a conviction for theft, is this ok? If a person has a conviction for domestic assault 5 years ago, is this ok? Putting a framework around acceptable criminal history will make it easy when you are in the moment of decision. Lastly, a background check is like a test. The result is not entirely comprehensive, it is a snapshot in time. The results are only valid for the day the databases are searched. Background checks for your key roles such as safety team members should be carried out at least once a year.

CREATE A TRAINING PROGRAM

You have your safety leader in place, you have defined roles and responsibilities, you've found the good people and are starting on your journey, but this is where the real work begins. Being a safety team member is a lot like being a pastor, deacon, clergy, or any other religious title you can think of. Once you have it, people start to look at you as a position of authority and expect that you know the answers to their questions. In England, we call it Sod's Law. Here in the United States, it's called Murphy's Law. Anything that can happen will happen! As soon as you announce to the church staff or congregation that a safety team exists, the calls and questions will come.

When I started my position at MOA I had only been in the country for eight weeks. There was a five-week training program where I was to shadow all the different teams and complete the basic training. Now even though my official title was Special Operations Captain, I did not wear the rank markings on my hat. Why? If people had seen me walking the floor of the largest retail-entertainment complex in the Mid-West, both security staff and mall guests would have looked to me for answers to questions that I might not have known. I completed my training in a uniform with no rank markings as to who I was, and I can tell you I'm grateful that I did as I wouldn't have been ready on day one to answer the questions that came with my authority.

You need to ensure that you are providing the right training, equipping, and empowering the people you take onto your team to be successful. I encourage all safety teams to take on people who have gone through some type of basic onboarding program such as the ones listed below. This list is not definitive but will help your team be set up for success.

» Church culture and mission

» Knowing the church leadership

» Church outreach programs

- » Security mission statement

- » Policies and procedures

- » Approved use of force continuum

- » Suspicious behavior training

- » Verbal de-escalation

- » Scenario training

- » Report writing

- » Basic medical response

- » Tour of the building(s)

- » Radio procedures

As soon as I put that Special Operations Captain uniform and badge on, people looked at me differently. When you walk the floor with a senior ranking officer wearing the rank, there is an assumed responsibility that you are who you say you are. If you are reading this and think you don't have the level of training you feel you need, take some personal responsibility and hunt down the people or organizations that can help.

Create a personal training plan, it's important to move through a cycle of discussion-based to real-life training scenarios. A common pathway to success is to try and follow this order in your training:

- » Attending church seminars

- » Attending workshops to improve learning

- » Conducting tabletop scenarios to answer the "what if" questions

- » Conducting drills such as fire alarm and active shooter

- » Functional exercises that lead to full-scale exercises with local law enforcement

The most effective learning will most often come from conducting drills. As someone new joins your team or if you'd like to gain individual knowledge, it is always important to go back to seminars and workshops.

STRIKING THE RIGHT BALANCE

It is often hard to get long term commitment form volunteers and sometimes we forget that these people are donating their time. When I started training and presenting at churches, I noticed that volunteers would either be missing or unable to attend because of personal and work commitments. These churches would go to a great expense to bring me into their community to educate and sometimes I would have to go back at another time and train those who couldn't make it. This wasn't effective for the churches or the volunteers.

I know a lot of churches mandate training, which is good but remember, these are volunteers. I worked with a church that had a solid and robust safety program. The team was longstanding, most serving for over three years. The security director moved on and so the church brought in a new head of security. Within four months, the entire 12-person team turned over and the church asked for my help as to why. Within a glance at their training program, it became obvious. They set a training standard which was almost impossible to achieve. You need to be mindful that the commitment to this team is two-sided; the volunteer has to be willing to volunteer time out of their busy schedules, and the organization has to be respectful of people's time when they set their requirements. Everyone has a breaking point. Nine times out of ten these people are not being paid; they are volunteers wanting to help. If you require them to come to two all-day trainings a month, you have to be considerate of their time as they may also be serving on a Sunday. Also, remember the objective of this is ministry. You are not training them to be tactical warriors, that is the role of the police. The safety team is to observe and report and those that are highly skilled such as the police officers on your teams can take action in violent and confrontational situations.

Determine what your key areas of training are such as the things your team cannot afford to miss out on! Look at these as your must-haves. Make these mandatory but discuss this with your team and those in other ministries before you make any announcements to make sure it aligns with your culture and commitment.

One way you can get engagement from your volunteers is to find interesting speakers, security experts, law enforcement officers, and agents. Even in a small church, you'll find these people within your communities that you can ask to share their knowledge. If you call your local law enforcement and ask to speak with their crime prevention or community officer, they may have recommendations for you.

CREATE TRAINING RECORDS

Other than taking the training itself, the second most important thing you can do is maintain good training records. Training records provide great governance by knowing what your team has completed and is helpful when tracking individual records. Having accurate records will support you if your program is ever tested through a complaint or litigation.

This can be tracked through sign-in sheets, SharePoint, or access databases. Here are some simple things you can do to start building up a strong governance program around your training records:

Ensure you have a way to record some of these documentation standards:

» Individual training records

» Sign-in sheets

» Incident reports

» Certification requirements

» Mandatory training

WORSHIP AT ONE, SERVE AT ANOTHER

You have your team. You're working hard to make everything run in unison together. You have structured some training using the resources that you have, and the team is operating on Sundays. I want to share something that I see around faith communities that I phrase "worship at one, serve at another". I have seen safety team members walk around the church drinking coffee, pray during the service, be involved in the service by singing and clapping, and be engrossed in the message that is being preached. All good things, EXCEPT when you're supposed to be keeping the congregation safe and are to be focused on observing and reporting. This is not any ordinary volunteer position. In this role, you are looking out for the safety of others. If you are closing your eyes to pray you cannot be situationally aware. If you are sipping your coffee you are distracted, and if you are sitting next to your family during the service and something happens, it will be your instinct to protect them from the danger, not the pastor or the congregation.

I have never seen the secret service protect the President of the United States with a coffee in their hand or a police officer attend a burglary call and take his wife and daughter with him into the house. I see many safety team members distracted. When serving, set aside an hour or so of your time dedicated to safety where you can be alert, attentive, and ready to respond. It's why I encourage safety team leaders to practice "worship at one, serve at another". If you want to go to the service with your partner and children and enjoy the music, then do so either before or after you serve. For that short window, the church wants you fulfilling the role of safety officer.

I recommend you look out for these behaviors in your safety team whilst they are serving, then hold the difficult conversations as to why they are not a good idea:

SPECIAL EVENT SECURITY

If we take the topic of mass shootings, most often we think about these occurring during worship hours. Carl Chinn spent many years collating statistics on deadly force incidents at houses of worship. Interestingly, most of these acts occurred outside of worship hours. The rate of risk increases when we are a place of mass gathering on Sunday, but I want to reiterate that as a church there are many risks outside of worship hours. Some examples include VBS, youth ministry, preschools, addiction clinics, divorce care classes, prison rehabilitation programs, Christmas concerts, guest speakers, public baptisms and funerals all of which might need consideration for security.

HAVING THE RIGHT EQUIPMENT

One thing that we haven't touched on yet is what equipment your safety team members should have. Firstly, it is a given that they should have some means of communication. Cell phones are a good baseline if you are at a small church, but the ideal standard is radios. Don't be embarrassed if you don't have something in place, you can get this up and running relatively cheaply. Costco, Sam's Club, and BestBuy have affordable two-way radios that you can buy earpieces for. The earpiece is an essential piece of equipment so that members can talk in private without alerting the congregation about a suspicious person, medical emergency, etc.

The other essential piece of equipment to have is a way for the safety team to defend themselves. The question of should they have pepper spray, handcuffs, or baton all comes down to the security culture of your environment and the mission of your team.

Here is my advice on firearms; mass shootings are low probability, high impact. I'll say it again, low probability, high impact. If an event were to ever occur at your church, what would you want the response to be? It's important to go back to step 2 (Implement a Safety Committee) on this and discuss with your safety committee what your response is going to be. If you determine you would want to carry firearms, here are some things to discuss:

» Have you ruled out all other options such as police on duty, police off duty, private security contractors?

» Do you have the right persons carrying at your church?

» Do you have the appropriate insurance coverage?

» Do you have documented minutes from your church board that a permit to carry is acceptable?

» Do you have an attorney on retainer, or one identified, should the need arise?

» Have you discussed any legal waiver signed by the safety team members against the church?

» Do you have a copy of the permit to carry certificates on file? (so you know they are lawful)

» Do you have a training standard?

» Are you holding safety team members to that standard?

» Have you reviewed the background of those carrying?

» Should you require eyesight tests?

» Do you know enough about the person's psychological disposition to approve them to carry

» Your local community and state laws as they pertain to firearms/weapons. Each state is different.

When that day of evil comes, and it will appear somewhere in your faith community, you want to be ready with a proactive response, whatever that looks like for your faith community. How will you stop the threat? If the church safety team are the ones to stop the threat, then these questions should be answered in detail with leadership before any person starts carrying on your premises. This is to protect you and the church from not only a safety standpoint but from reputational risk and legal action should something ever go wrong.

FINAL WORDS

I know that through all the 7 steps there are many challenges and hurdles that you will need to overcome. Everything written here is easier said than done but I have used this process at hundreds of churches across many faith dominations. This is a macro book designed to engage conversation, provide you with call to action tasks, and most importantly help determine what each of these steps look like in your faith community. When I wrote this book, I did so with you in mind, knowing how daunting safety can be for those who do not do this full time, do not have the support or struggle knowing where to start. Firstly, you are not alone. My prayer is that this may be a guide for you on your journey, taking each concept one step at a time. Many have walked in your shoes and I encourage you to reach out to others in your community to discuss ideas, feelings, and thoughts.

Remember, until I spoke with my pastor on safety one day by chance, I never considered security to be a ministry. God called me to serve and share the experiences He has provided me with. Although the 7 steps are laid out in an order where I feel they will give you the best opportunity to successfully start a program, many of you might have completed a little bit of each step, and that's ok. I pray this will provide you an intentional road map to build a stronger foundation to be successful. Take what works in your faith community and do what you can to plan, prepare, and protect!

God Bless!

Simm

NOTES

BOOK NOTES

—

SCRIPTURE

All scripture in this book is from the American Standard Bible and is publicly available free online. With many different versions of the bible available you may have a different translated version than me. I do not believe that these different translations will affect the meaning of my use.

INTRODUCTION

1. For those wanting to learn more about Mall of America, you can Google or search it out on Wikipedia. There are some interesting articles about the program that I used to oversee. These cover how public perception can shape and influence reputational risk and the growth of suspicious behavior programs. I always love to hear stories you can contact me at info@kingswoodsc.com to let me know your reflections.

"Under Suspicion at the Mall of America". NPR. September 7, 2011

"Be particularly careful' today, U.S. homeland security chief tells MOA visitors". Star Tribune. 22 February 2015. Retrieved 22 February 2015.

2. There are many news sources where you can find information on Dylann Roof if you would like to learn more. I would suggest this CNN report for well-balanced reporting.

"Charleston church shooting: Who is Dylann Roof?" CNN December 16, 2006

If you are interested in listening to part of his video confession with the FBI, the Wall Street Journal YouTube Channel has an abstract of the interview available free online. Search Dylann Roof Admits to Church Shooting in Video Recording (December 12, 2016) on the WSJ YouTube Channel.

3. Many of you might not know Carl Chinn, but he is an incredibly well-respected figure in the world of church safety. It's worth checking out his organization the Faith Based Security Network. It has a daily forum and shares best practices from across the country in security ministry. His website can be found at fbsnamerica.com.

STEP 1 IDENTIFY YOUR SECURITY CULTURE
1. Mark 1:23

[23] Just then there was a man in their synagogue with an unclean spirit; and he cried out, [24] saying, "What business do we have with each other, Jesus of Nazareth? Have You come to destroy us? I know who You are—the Holy One of God!" [25] And Jesus rebuked him, saying, "Be quiet, and come out of him!" [26] Throwing him into convulsions, the unclean spirit cried out with a loud voice and came out of him. [27] They were all amazed, so that they debated among themselves, saying, "What is this? A new teaching

with authority! He commands even the unclean spirits, and they obey Him."

2. John 7:1

[1] After these things Jesus was walking in Galilee, for He was unwilling to walk in Judea because the Jews were seeking to kill Him. [2] Now the feast of the Jews, the Feast of Booths, was near. [3] Therefore His brothers said to Him, "Leave here and go into Judea, so that Your disciples also may see Your works which You are doing. [4] For no one does anything in secret when he himself seeks to be known publicly. If You do these things, show Yourself to the world.

3. I had the unique opportunity to interview Frank Pomeroy about his life before the tragic events at First Baptist Church, and how it shaped the community afterward. If you are interested in learning more on his personal journey you can listen to the full conversation by going to the following platforms.

» For the video, interview visit "Simon Osamoh" on YouTube

» Facebook https://www.facebook.com/WhoIBecame/

» Search "Who I Became" within Apple Podcasts, Spotify and iHeart Radio

STEP 2 IMPLEMENT A SAFETY COMMITTEE

In 1983 Steve Jobs Founder of Apple gave a speech at the International Design Conference in Aspen. It is here where we first heard him say "we hire people to tell us what to do". If you want to listen to the full speech go to YouTube and type in Steve Jobs International Design Conference or Steve Jobs "We hire people to tell us what to do" where you can listen to the full audio.

STEP 3 PROTECT YOUR PERIMETER

1. If you aren't familiar with the Trojan Horse story, there are many sources online. Start with the Britannica encyclopedia at https://www.britannica.com/topic/Trojan-horse

2. To learn more about the ISIS Church attack in France, the BBC have some good reporting

France church attack: Priest killed by two 'IS militants, BBC 26 July 2016

3. If you are interested in learning more about layers of security/circles of security, you will find many articles and downloads available online. Use the keyword ASIS. Meaning American Society for Industrial Security. They are one of the largest security organizations in the world and have many reputable papers and information on the subject.

4 Peter 5:8

[8] Be of sober spirit, be on the alert. Your adversary, the devil, prowls around like a roaring lion, seeking someone to devour.

5. Jimmy Meeks from Sheepdog Seminars https://www.sheepdogsafetytraining.com/

6. Lt Col (Retired) Dave Grossman's organization Killogy can be found here https://www.killology.com/

7. To view the lawsuit filed by the families against the firearms manufacturers Bushmaster Firearms International LLC search Google Sandy Hook Families Compliant

STEP 4 CONDUCT A SECURITY ASSESSMENT

1. My organization Kingswood Security Consulting LLC specializes in helping soft targets and nonprofits improve security measures and formulate action plans through security assessments. More on Kingswood Security can be found by visiting Kingswoodsc.com

2. Luke 20:21

[21] They questioned Him, saying, "Teacher, we know that You speak and teach correctly, and You are not partial to any, but teach the way of God in truth. [22] Is it lawful for us to pay taxes to Caesar, or not?" [23] But He detected their trickery and said to them, [24] "Show Me a denarius. Whose likeness and inscription does it have?" They said, "Caesar's." [25] And He said to them, "Then render to Caesar the things that are Caesar's, and to God the things that are God's."

STEP 5 WRITE POLICY AND PROCEDURES

1. I mention my friend Tina Rowe who I have learned a lot from over the years on security ministry. She has a lot of publicly available information that is free to download by checking out her website http://tinalewisrowe.com/ I had the honor to video interview Tina where she talks about her "what could go wrong" concept. These videos and several others of her speaking can be found on the Worship Security Association website at Worshipsecurity.org

2. There are many run hide fight resources available online. It is quite a simple concept with a few variations. I would look at resources from DHS Department of Homeland Security (DHS) or the video Run Hide Fight which can be downloaded from WSA.

I've got to know Kris Moloney of Sheepdog Church Security who is also based here in Minneapolis MN. He has a beginner's resource available on active shooter mitigation which is available through Amazon Active Shooter Mitigation: A Training Guide for Houses of Worship

STEP 6 CONDUCT SAFETY TRAINING

1. My 4 rules of suspicious behavior are featured in the online video class "Responding to Suspicious Behavior" available to purchase through the WSA site.

2. I mentioned Special Agent friend Joe Bezotte. Joe spends time outside of his work as a federal agent running personal perseveration classes. His website is https://coresecuritymn.com/

3. The hot topic right now is verbal de-escalation. John Riley from Michigan is the founder of Gentle Response and he travels the country teaching verbal de-escalation to churches, small business-es, and police departments. He's one of the best out there and his website can be found at http://gentle-response.com/

STEP 7 START A SAFETY TEAM

1. Exodus 18

You will surely wear out, both yourself and these people who are with you, for the task is too heavy for you; you cannot do it alone.

2. The Church Safety Guys are a nonprofit organization who work primarily on Facebook. There Facebook Group "Church Safety & Security" group has around 3,000 members and it's a great way to connect with likeminded people and receive free information on the best way to start or maintain a safety team.

3. Luke 5:8

[8] But when Simon Peter saw that, he fell down at Jesus' feet, saying, "Go away from me Lord, for I am a sinful man!" [9] For amazement had seized him and all his companions because of the catch of fish which they had taken; [10] and so also were James and John, sons of Zebedee, who were partners with Simon. And Jesus said to Simon, "Do not fear, from now on you will be catch-ing men." [11] When they had brought their boats to land, they left everything and followed Him.

NOTES

ABOUT THE AUTHOR

—

Simon Osamoh

FOUNDER AND DIRECTOR

Founder of Kingswood Security Consulting and the Worship Security Association (WSA). He is a recognized organized crime, terrorism and faith security specialist, Simon spent 14 years as a Detective in England working serious and organized crime. In 2006 he worked with the British security services into the Investigation of the "liquid bomb terrorism plot" against the U.S, which changed aviation security worldwide.

He is a former Security Manager at Mall of America, Minnesota where he oversaw counterterrorism and the internationally-recognized behavior detection program. Former Vice President for the FBI Minneapolis Citizens Academy Alumni Association, former program chair of InfraGard Minnesota.

He holds an Individualized B.A focused on British American criminal justice and is a member of Westwood Community Church in Excelsior Minnesota, where he has served as security advisor since 2013.

The author of the books *Securing Church Operations A Seven Step Plan For Ministry & Safety Leaders* and *Responding To Suspicious Behavior* and the host of the Who I Became Podcast.

Made in the USA
Monee, IL
02 November 2024

69151438R00090